Who Am Eye?

THE QUESTION IS NOT ONLY 'WHO AM I?' BUT 'WHOSE AM I?

DR. JOHAN GREEN

Scripture Permissions

Published by Learn Live Hope Journey LLC

www.learnlivehopejourney.com

Printed in the United States of America

Library of Congress Control Number: 2025914964

Contents

Acknowledgements

Who am Eye?

First and foremost, I acknowledge the One in whom my identity is rooted: To Jesus Christ, I am eternally thankful for Your perfect sacrifice, for taking my place on the cross, and for calling me Your own. To the One who knows my heart, calls me by name, and never gives up on me—Jesus Christ, my Redeemer, my Restorer, my reason for hope.

To God the Father, thank You for being the kind of Father I could trust—whose unfailing love sustained me in every season of life.

To the Holy Spirit, Your abiding presence is real, Your guidance is true, Your comfort is healing, and You continue to show me who I am. You have been my Comforter, my Conviction, and my Constant Companion every step of the way.

Since 2005, this book has been a journey of discovering who God says I truly am. His lens is perfect—and through Jesus, I now see myself with greater clarity and grace.

I thank the Lord for His delays, teaching me that He will never give up on me. His purpose in trials, is to teach us that Jehovah keeps His promises, and Elohim displays His power to keep those promises, bringing resolution in His perfect time. God never delays without purpose, and He desires that we come to Him just as we are—with complete honesty.

Family and Personal Support

To my American parents, Billy and Linda Kivela—thank you for your unconditional love and support during my transition from South Africa to America, when I belonged fully to neither country, yet was learning to call both home.

To my mother, Alice, your faithful prayers and dedication helped me finally complete my doctorate and many other achievements in my life. I will never forget your strength and support, Mom. The love of many has grown cold, but yours has only increased—for me and our family. You are a tower of strength and honesty.

To my children, thank you for your love and grace, even during seasons when I could not be physically and emotionally present. I look forward to our years ahead, to see how God continues to shape our family.

Mentors and Spiritual Fathers

To Dr. Rob Reimer, thank you for your spiritual wisdom that shaped much of how I lead and write. Thank you for introducing me to Soul Care and the power of God's deliverance.

To Dr. Martin Saunders, now with the Lord, your deep insights remain with me still. Thank you for saying "You're in!" when I applied to the Doctor of Ministry program with Nyack College in 2014. But most of all, thank you for saying, "It matters not what people say to you, but what truly matters is what people say about you after you have left the room!"

To Pastor Trevor Walker, your authentic walk with Christ has profoundly impacted my life. Your presence was and is a constant invitation to draw closer to Jesus. I will never forget when you said, "Johan, God does not see you through your problems—He is above our problems."

To My Readers and Community

To every reader picking up this book, thank you for your willingness to engage with truth, vulnerability, and hope. May the Holy Spirit meet you on every page.

To every person who poured into my life during the writing of this book—friends, mentors, and readers—you helped me see what God was forming through these words. Thank you for believing in the process, for walking with me through my valleys, and for reflecting His love back to me when I needed it most.

To my family—you are part of every sentence, every prayer, and every healing breakthrough shared in these pages. I love you deeply.

To those whose stories are echoed in these pages, whether directly or through the heart of shared wounds and triumphs—you are not alone. This book is for you.

May the words you've read open new doors to grace, courage, and freedom.

This book represents the first part of a larger journey—discovering who you are leads naturally to understanding whose you are and why you're here. May this be the beginning of your most authentic chapter yet.

With gratitude,

—Dr. Johan Green

Introduction

When The Question Became The Journey

The question is not simply 'Who am I?' but 'Whose am I?

This book did not begin in a classroom or a church—it began on a sidewalk. I had just lost everything. My home had been repossessed. My vehicle was gone. My identity as a successful businessman had been stripped away. I was walking to the store when a car drove by—friends of mine. I lifted my hand to wave. They saw me. They knew me. But they turned their heads and drove on. The shame that rushed over me in that moment was so heavy I could hardly breathe.

That day, I asked the question that would define the rest of my life: "Lord, who am I?"

I was no longer the rich kid or the guy with the title. I was just Johan—barefoot in identity, standing on nothing but grace.

What I didn't know then was that I was exactly where I

needed to be for God to begin His deepest work.

Ever since, I have been discovering that the greatest discoveries in life don't come through achievement—they come through surrender. As I lost everything, I began to see more clearly what could never be taken from me: my identity in Christ.

But here's what took me years to understand, and what I pray this book will help you discover much sooner: the moment of devastating loss wasn't the beginning of my story—it was the beginning of my real story. The story God had been writing all along, beneath the layers of performance, beneath the false securities, beneath the identities I had constructed to protect myself from exactly this kind of pain.

The Foundation of True Identity

In the beginning, God created—intentionally, intricately, and in His image. This foundational truth in Genesis 1 isn't merely theological—it is deeply personal. To be made in the Imago Dei means we were created to reflect the heart and holiness of our Creator. Our purpose flows not from what we do, but from who He is, and who we are in Him.

The Hebrew name for God in Genesis 1 is Elohim, which means "Almighty Creator" or "Putter-forth of energy." The word used for create is bara, meaning to create out of nothing. This creative act was not random—it was relational. When God said, "Let Us make man in Our image" (Genesis 1:26, ASV), He used the word asah—to fashion or shape. Together, these words reveal that we are both formed and filled, designed with intention and breathed into by the Spirit.

To understand ourselves rightly, we must return to this original truth: You were made by God, for God, and in God's image. That image, though marred by sin, has been restored completely through Christ. This book is a journey back to the True Self—who you were created to be before life, lies, and wounds distorted your reflection.

The Imago Dei within you is not lost—it's being rediscovered as you shed the false identities that never belonged to you and embrace the True Self, that has always been secure in Christ.

You may ask, "Who am I?" But God already answered: very good. (Genesis 1:31, ASV)

My Own Journey: From Questions to Quest

This book was born from my own questions, wrestlings, wounds, and slow awakenings. It wasn't written in a weekend retreat or a writing workshop—it came from years of asking God, "Who am I really?" and being patient enough to wait for the answers.

Over time, those questions began to shift. I realized that the journey was not just about discovering myself—but about discovering the One who made me. The deeper shift moved me away from self-centered searching toward a God-centered knowing. From, "Who am I?" to, "Whose am I?"—because knowing Whose I am revealed more about who I am, than anything else.

This distinction between "Who am I?" and "Whose am I?" became the cornerstone of my entire identity transformation.

"Who am I?" focuses on self-discovery, achievements, roles, and personal characteristics. It asks: What do I do? What are my talents? How do others see me? What have I accomplished? This question, while important, can lead us into endless introspection and performance-based identity.

"Whose am I?" shifts the focus to belonging, relationship, and divine ownership. It asks: Who created me? Who loves me unconditionally? Who calls me by name? To whom do I belong? This question anchors our identity in something unshakeable—God's unchanging love and eternal purpose.

The profound truth is this: when you know whose you are, you begin to discover who you are. Your identity flows from your relationship with the One who made you, not from your achievements, failures, or the opinions of others.

And it was there—in the arms of the Father—that I began to find peace, healing, and clarity. I continue to learn who God says I am—and each day, I uncover more of my identity as His beloved.

That single question on the sidewalk turned into a pilgrimage. I discovered that the journey of identity is not about constructing something new—it's about uncovering what's already there. God had already written my name in His book, but the layers of loss, betrayal, unforgiveness, and emotional pain had formed a warped lens that distorted this truth. I desperately needed to believe—not just know—that my name was written in the book of life. There was a disconnect between my heart and my mind. I knew about salvation, but I didn't fully believe it with all my heart. My head had the theology, but my soul was still searching for home.

The Breakthrough That Changed Everything

One of my professors once said to me, "Johan, you have many pearls, but in this assignment, you failed to bring them together on the string." Something inside me clicked. God wasn't just handing me truth—He was stringing it together into wisdom, helping me see through His lens rather than my warped perspective, shaped by years of wounds. Pearls are found deep in the ocean and are forged under pressure. And like pearls, your identity is formed in the deep places—the places where grace presses against the wounds of your past. Fortunately, God gave me a second chance to allow Him to bring it all together.

I am eternally grateful for that professor's honesty—and even more grateful to the God who makes beauty out of brokenness.

But the real breakthrough came when I stopped trying to figure out who I was and started learning who God said I was. When I stopped looking in the mirror of my circumstances, and started looking in the mirror of His Word. When I stopped defining myself by my failures and started receiving my identity from His faithfulness.

That's when everything changed. Not overnight—transformation is a process, not an event—but consistently, surely, powerfully.

This shift from self-discovery to divine revelation, became the foundation for everything that followed. It changed not just how I saw myself, but how I approached every relationship, every challenge, every opportunity that came my way.

Why This Book Exists: An Invitation to Your True Self

I'm not offering answers as much as I'm offering companionship. You'll read stories from my life, insights from mentors and theologians, and reflections born in the dark night of the soul. These are not abstract ideas. They are hard-won truths that I pray will encourage you. You are not alone. And you are not broken beyond repair.

God sees you. God hears you. And more than anything, God desires to connect with your heart—just as much as we need to connect with the heart of our Creator. Because in doing so,

He shows us who we truly are.

This is not just a book—it is a testimony and prayer of personal surrender. A sacred invitation to open your heart, not only to information, but to transformation.

This book is for the person who feels unseen, who has tried to define themselves by success, relationships, or performance—and has still come up empty. It's for the exhausted achiever who has climbed every ladder, only to discover they were leaning against the wrong wall. It's for the people-pleaser who has worn so many masks they've forgotten their own face. It's for the wounded soul who believes their pain disqualifies them from God's love.

It's for the one who's tired of wearing a mask and ready to be known.

It's for the believer who has walked with God but still feels unsure of who they are.

It's for anyone who has ever stood in front of a mirror and wondered, "Is this really me?"

But most of all, this book is for the person who is brave enough to ask the question that changes everything: "Who am Eye?"

Your Sacred Invitation: The Journey Ahead

The chapters that follow are more than teachings—they are invitations. Each one invites you to:

- Reflect deeply
- Surrender honestly
- Reclaim your God-given identity
- Walk in healing, freedom, and purpose

This journey unfolds in sacred stages. We begin by learning to listen—to God's voice and your own soul. We then explore how your body, soul, and spirit each play vital roles in your identity formation. You'll discover the Four Selves—Actual, False, Presentable, and True—as we walk through layers of pain, performance, belief, and identity, learning to release what was never yours, and embrace who you've always been in Christ. Finally, we'll explore how healed identity transforms your relationships, your purpose, and your daily walk with God.

You will hear your own story echoed in the stories of Scripture. And most of all, I pray that you will encounter the One who sees you, knows you, and calls you His own.

My prayer is that through the testimony and words in this book, lives will be transformed. That through this unfolding journey, readers will feel invited into a relationship with the One who never gave up on them—the One who has been pursuing you long before you ever thought to seek Him.

The Four Selves: A Framework for Transformation

Throughout this journey, you'll discover that different versions of yourself show up, depending on where you are spiritually and what life is throwing at you. I call these the Four Selves:

Your Actual Self - The beautiful, messy reality of being human. This is you without filters, acknowledging both your brokenness and your belovedness, your struggles and your strengths.

Your False Self - The wounded you, operating from fear and pain, using strategies that once helped you survive, but now sabotage your ability to thrive.

Your Presentable Self - The curated you, carefully

managing impressions and avoiding vulnerability, to maintain an image you think others want to see.

Your True Self - The Christ-formed you, secure in God's love and naturally expressing His character through your unique personality and gifts.

The goal isn't to eliminate the other selves—they're part of the human experience. The goal is to live more consistently from your True Self, the person who God created you to be before wounds, performance, and fear distorted your reflection.

What Makes This Journey Different

This isn't another self-help book. It's not a theological argument. It's a journey—a map for those who are brave enough to ask the question that changes everything: "Who am Eye?"

This book was born from real life, not theory. From sitting with a couple whose marriage was falling apart, from praying with a man who'd lost his job and his confidence, from my own 4 AM wrestling matches with God, when nothing made sense.

You see, I've spent years watching people (including myself) try to figure out why they keep doing things they don't want to do. Why they feel like strangers to themselves sometimes. Why they can love Jesus deeply, but still struggle with the same patterns over and over.

This framework emerged from those real conversations, those honest prayers, and the beautiful messiness of actual transformation.

A Note Before You Begin

This book is not a one-time read. It's a companion for the soul.

Every chapter offers space for reflection, questions to draw you deeper, and a call to action that invites change. It is best read slowly, with an open heart and a listening posture.

As you journey through "Who Am Eye," you are invited to deepen your transformation by using The Four Selves Discovery Exercise located in Appendix A. You may also wish to use the Companion Journal reflection exercises in Appendix D.

For those seeking ongoing community and support in this journey, you're warmly invited to connect with our Learn Live Hope Journey family at learnlivehopejourney.info. There you'll find additional spiritual formation resources, opportunities to join our weekly live podcast for identity-focused Q&A sessions, and access to our growing library of recorded teachings on YouTube. Whether you're part of a local church community or walking this path individually, you're never alone in your transformation journey.

Important Disclaimer

Before we begin this transformative journey together, please refer to the full disclaimer in Appendix E for complete details. "Who Am Eye?" is designed for spiritual formation and growth within a Christian framework. This content represents biblical principles and pastoral guidance, not psychological counseling, mental health treatment, or professional therapy.

If you are experiencing mental health concerns, persistent depression, anxiety, thoughts of self-harm, or psychological distress, please seek help from qualified licensed mental health professionals. This book is intended to support your spiritual journey alongside, not in place of, appropriate professional care when needed.

The Journey and the Process

Here's what I want you to know before we begin: You are not an accident. You are not a mistake. You are not too broken, too wounded, or too far gone. You are God's masterpiece, being transformed day by day into the image of Christ.

The journey ahead won't always be comfortable, but it will be worth it. Because on the other side of acknowledged pain is authentic freedom. On the other side of named wounds is genuine wholeness. And on the other side of surrendered brokenness is the True Self that Christ has been forming in you all along.

Take your time. Reflect honestly. And let God's Spirit do a deep work within you.

And more than anything, remember this truth that will anchor everything we explore together: You are beloved. Not because of what you do, but because of whose you are. The God who created you, who knows every hair on your head, who bottles every tear—He is not disappointed in you. He is not surprised by your struggles. He is not shocked by your questions.

He is for you. He is with you. And He is transforming you into the person He always intended you to be.

Welcome to the journey of discovering who you really are.

Chapter 1

LISTEN TO HEAR THE HEART

"The Word of Scripture should never stop sounding in your ears and working in you all day long, just like the words of someone you love. And just as you do not analyze the words of someone you love, but accept them as they are said to you, accept the Word of Scripture and ponder it in your heart, as Mary did. That is all... Do not ask 'How shall I pass this on?' but 'What does it say to me?' Then ponder this word long in your heart until it has gone right into you and taken possession of you."

Dietrich Bonhoeffer

Bonhoeffer understood something that took me years to discover in my own journey—that the deepest transformation doesn't come from analyzing God's voice like a puzzle to solve, but from receiving it like a love letter meant just for you. Whether you're reading this in a church pew, a coffee shop, or your kitchen table at 2 AM wondering who you really are, this truth remains: God has something specific He wants to say about your identity, and He's been waiting for you to slow down long enough to hear it.

From This Journey Forward

Have you ever participated in one of those conversations where you felt totally seen and understood? While other conversations left you feeling misunderstood? The difference often isn't in what's said—it's in how we listen.

As we begin this exploration of whose you are, here's something that might surprise you: the secret to discovering who you really are isn't found by looking deeper into yourself, but by learning to truly listen. This simple practice of listening to hear the heart will become the foundation for everything we uncover together, about your identity in Christ.

Think about it: how much does a loving parent know about their child that the child hasn't discovered yet? What dreams, gifts, and possibilities does a father see in his son or daughter that they can't see in themselves? There's something in all of us—that curious inner child—that still wonders who we really are and who we're becoming.

Our heavenly Father holds those answers, and He's eager to share them with us, if we'll just learn to listen.

Bonhoeffer's wisdom points us toward this truth: just as we receive the words of someone we love without analyzing them to death, we must learn to receive God's words and His voice with the same trusting, open heart. When we ponder His truth long enough, it doesn't just inform us—it transforms us from the inside out.

Why This Chapter Matters

Before we can answer with honesty, clarity, or conviction, we must first learn to listen—to hear the heart of our heavenly Father.

God's heart as our Father is to know His children intimately. Just as a loving parent delights in hearing his child's voice and sharing his heart, God yearns for that same connection with us. When someone feels heard, they feel valued.

The same is true with God. He longs for you to hear His heart just as He listens to yours. His Father-heart beats with love for you, and in that sacred exchange of listening, something whispers—you begin to remember who you are and who you are in His love.

Listening is the forgotten gateway to identity. It slows down the world long enough for our soul to be heard—and for God's voice to be received. In a culture of noise, performance, and pressure, listening calls us back to the sacred rhythm of stillness. The journey toward discovering who you are begins with learning to recognize the voice that had been calling your name all along.

The Invitation to Listen

In the search for identity, we often start by looking for answers. But the real journey begins not with striving or speaking, but with stillness and listening.

Listening is more than a skill—it is a sacred act of connection. It opens your heart to God, to others, and to yourself. In quietness, we begin to hear what the noise of life often drowns out: the whisper of God and the cry of our soul. Rather than chasing identity, listening helps us receive it.

This is beautifully illustrated in the life of Samuel. As a young boy serving in the temple, he hears his name called in the night. Thinking it was Eli, he ran to him. But Eli discerns it was the Lord and tells him to respond: "Speak, Lord, for thy servant heareth' (1 Samuel 3:9).

That moment of stillness and surrender marks the beginning of Samuel's divine calling. Long before he became a prophet, he became a listener. Identity was awakened—not through performance, but through attention.

But here's what I've learned through years of asking the wrong questions: we often exhaust ourselves looking for identity in all the wrong places—achievements, relationships, success, even ministry—when the answer has been waiting in the quiet place where God speaks our name.

Samuel felt heard when God responded to his invitation. He felt known when God called his name—not once, but twice: "Samuel! Samuel!" That's the power of listening. It makes us feel seen, known, and deeply loved. And God still calls your name. He longs to hear you call on Him. He has a specific identity and purpose that He is waiting to share with you.

God's heart as our Father is to know His children intimately. Just as a loving father delights in hearing his child's voice and sharing his heart, God yearns for that same connection with us. When someone feels heard, they feel valued.

The same is true with God. He longs for you to hear His heart just as He listens to yours. His Father-heart beats with love for you, and in that sacred exchange of listening, something whispers—you begin to remember whose you are and who you are in His love.

This chapter invites you to slow down, breathe, and open your heart. Like Samuel, in the quiet of night, may you whisper, "Speak, Lord." And posture your heart to hear. You are being called—not to perform, but to listen. As you tune your ear to God's voice, you will begin to rediscover the identity He planted in you.

When We Listen, Who's Leading?

Samuel's transformation shows us that we all have different ways of listening, depending on which part of ourselves is leading the conversation. His journey from confused boy to confident prophet illustrates how our listening evolves as we mature spiritually.

Young Samuel: When he first heard God's voice, he was confused and kept running to Eli. He hadn't yet learned to recognize the Father's voice calling his name. His listening was reactive and uncertain.

Learning Samuel: With Eli's wise guidance, he learnt to say "Speak, Lord! for thy servant heareth." This was the turning point—Samuel learnt to listen from surrender rather than fear. He stopped running and started receiving.

Mature Samuel: Later in life, Samuel heard God's voice clearly about anointing kings and delivering difficult messages. His listening had become confident and clear because he knew whose voice he was hearing.

We'll explore Samuel's complete journey through different aspects of identity more deeply in Chapter 5, where his story perfectly illustrates the Four Selves framework.

God often does the same with us. We run to people because God doesn't feel real to us yet. We seek advice from friends, counsel from mentors, validation from those around us—all good things, but sometimes we're running when we should be listening. There comes a time to stop running to people and listen for the voice of God. Samuel had to learn that the voice calling his name wasn't Eli's—it was his heavenly Father's.

As we learn to listen deeply, something beautiful happens: we start recognizing which part of ourselves is showing up in the moment. Sometimes our wounded parts want to have the last word, ready to defend and protect. Sometimes our people-pleasing parts take over, becoming whoever we think others want us to be instead of who we really are. Sometimes our raw, honest parts hear everything but haven't learned how to respond with wisdom yet. But when our truest self leads—the part of us that's secure in God's love—we can listen with Christ's heart: patient, peaceful, and strong enough to truly hear without needing to fix or defend.

Learning to listen from our truest self is essential to discovering who we really are in God's eyes. It's the difference between defensive listening and grace-filled listening.

The Discipline of Not Having the Last Word

One of the most powerful forms of listening I've learned, comes from Dallas Willard's teaching on not needing to have the last word. In "Living in Christ's Presence," he reminds us that every moment is an opportunity to be with our Teacher. This practice of sacred restraint is actually a form of deep listening—choosing to hear rather than immediately respond.

He once said: "The truth is that I have my own set of struggles. But I am actually living in the reality of the kingdom. That reality is taking over my body in ways I want it to take over."

Another time he remarked: "I often feel stressed. But I am actually living in the reality of the gospel when I stop needing to control every outcome."

That kind of surrender begins with listening. True listening means we release the need to be right, to speak first, or to fix everything. When we let go of control, we create sacred space for the Holy Spirit to speak.

Jesus modeled this beautifully. When people challenged Him, He didn't rush to defend Himself. He responded with questions, parables, or silence. He practiced listening with divine restraint. His presence and posture spoke louder than any argument.

This same surrender begins with listening. True listening means we release the need to be right, to speak first, or to fix everything. When we let go of control, we create sacred space for the Holy Spirit to speak.

I've learned this lesson painfully in my own family. There was a time when my children would say to me, "Dad, you always seem angry." I'd respond defensively: "I'm not angry!" But my posture was communicating something different. What they were sensing wasn't anger, but stress. I was trying to control the outcome of life with my tone, my tension, and my presence. I hadn't yet realized that my body was speaking what my soul hadn't surrendered.

The Holy Spirit showed me that true peace comes from surrender, not control. Sometimes the most powerful word is no word at all—just grace-filled presence. This was my journey from reactive listening to receptive listening.

Listening in Our Homes

When people always have the last word, others in their lives begin to feel that there's no point in speaking because what they say won't make a difference. This is how we lose connection in our closest relationships—not through big blowups, but through the slow erosion of hope that we can actually be heard.

But the problem goes deeper than just needing the last word. Too many relationships suffer not from a lack of love, but from a lack of real listening. A person can hear words but miss the heart—because we are often too distracted by what we assume they mean instead of truly hearing what's being said.

The result is devastating. Sometimes, people live under

the same roof but feel completely disconnected. One partner checks out emotionally, even while staying physically present. When someone doesn't feel heard, they slowly begin to shut down and disconnect emotionally. I often remind couples: You don't need a divorce decree to be divorced at the heart.

This is why the discipline of restraint becomes so vital in our relationships. When we learn to listen to understand rather than to respond, we create connection instead of disconnection. We create healing instead of hurt.

Communication often gets stuck in correcting statements instead of connecting with sentiments. Years ago, van der Merwe trained me in Imago Relationship Facilitation, teaching me how to listen to hear the heart. That experience changed the way I approach relationships and pastoral care. It showed me that most people speak from a place of longing, love, or unmet needs.

The simple phrase "Tell me more" can be so powerful and that a flame of deepened connection could ignite. These three words create safety. They say: "I want to understand you—not fix you, not argue with you, but really hear you."

Another practical tool is mirroring—simply repeating back what you hear someone say. It sounds simple, but when someone pours out years of emotion in one long sentence, it becomes overwhelming. That's when I guide couples to slow down. "Let's try one thought at a time," I say. And when that single thought is mirrored back, something sacred happens. The sender feels heard—maybe for the first time.

Learning to listen well in our human relationships prepares us for the deeper work of listening to God. As we learn to truly hear people's hearts and not just their words, something shifts in our relationship with God too. We become more able to receive what our heavenly Father wants to speak over our identity. Too often we approach Him with our agenda—a list of things to say—instead of simply showing up to listen.

Listening for God's Voice

Once we've learned to listen well to others, we can apply those same principles to hearing our heavenly Father. Listening for the voice of God is more than hearing audible words. It's about becoming attuned to the still, small whisper, that speaks beneath the noise.

Listening is an act of surrender. It's choosing to believe that God still speaks—and that what He says is more important than what we want to say.

In my own life, the moments that have transformed me most were not when I spoke—but when I finally stopped to listen.

This is where memorizing just one Bible verse at a time becomes powerful. Not for the sake of performance, but as a doorway to presence. After you memorize the verse, ask the Holy Spirit: "Tell me more." It's in that sacred space that the Spirit begins to reveal what your soul needs to hear.

Recently, the Holy Spirit spoke to me through Mark 15:7: "The man called Barabbas was imprisoned with the insurrectionists who had committed murder in the civil rebellion." At first, I read it and moved on. But something stirred. The Spirit prompted me: "Go back. Ask again."

So I whispered: "Tell me more." I sensed the Lord guiding me to look deeper. I remembered that Barabbas means "son of the father." That name—so ordinary—was shouting something profound. There was a sense of belonging in it.

Barabbas: the criminal, the one sentenced to die, was still seen as a son.

As I asked again, "Tell me more," I felt a holy whisper: Barabbas was condemned by human law, but 2,000 years ago, God saw a son who would be pardoned by his Father.

In that moment, God wasn't just telling me about Barabbas. He was reminding me of myself. God's heart as our Father is to see us first as His children, regardless of our past, our failures, or our condemnation.

Even when we feel most unworthy, His Father-heart sees a beloved son or daughter who belongs to Him.

This is what happens when we listen—not just to Scripture, but to the Spirit who still speaks through it.

Listening to Ourselves

As we grow in our ability to listen to others and to God, we must also learn the delicate art of listening to our own hearts. When I was a child, my mom would often say: "Johan, you don't listen." The truth is that I often didn't listen. There was a part of me that didn't always want to hear the truth. But doesn't this ring true for all of us?

One of the responsibilities of being a parent is to speak truth to your child when the child is not willing to be honest with themselves.

My mom would say: "I'm not going to tell you what you want to hear—I'm going to tell you the truth."

Listening becomes the sacred bridge where healing flows between head and heart. There's often a disconnect between the mind and the heart, but our spiritual ears help us connect what we know intellectually with what our hearts need to believe. Somewhere in between the head and the heart lies truth. That absolute truth is only found when we are willing to be honest with ourselves and take that honesty to the throne of grace.

Sometimes, I have to say my own name: "Johan." In the Greek, Johan is connected to the meaning of "God is gracious." And I believe God gave me that name on purpose—because grace is something I need to receive daily. Especially with those closest to me.

The truth is: I sometimes struggle to consistently be gracious to those I love most, because I've been deeply wounded by those who were closest to me. God's heart as our Father understands our struggles with grace, especially toward those meant to protect us, and His Father-heart aches with us.

The Father knows that we are more than victorious, that we should be prospering in these relationships.

Sometimes when I've caught myself in a moment of heaviness, I've stood in front of a mirror and simply forced myself to smile. That small, intentional act—combining with a pause—can change my internal dialogue and give me perspective. It's in those moments that I hear my soul say: "Johan, it's going to be OK. Stress isn't your master—Jesus is Master."

But we must be intentional about believing this truth. It's easy to stay stuck in our own heads, overthinking, carrying stress, and never truly stepping out of our mental spiral of self-doubt and disbelief. We need to create moments that are light and joyful—on purpose—simply reminding ourselves that all things are possible with God.

When I truly open my ears to hear what the Spirit is saying, I come into alignment with my truest self—the version of me that is formed in grace, not fear. Our spiritual ears are the gateway to our soul, the place where we carry our emotional wounds. Listening becomes a sacred act of surrender, aligning our hearts with the truth of who God says we are.

It's a fine balance: to choose joy, to embrace life's goodness, and also to listen when the soul needs to be heard. This balance is critical to soul care.

When God Seems Silent in Our Pain

But what about those seasons when we're finally brave enough to feel, but God seems silent? These quiet times are often where the deepest growth happens, and they're part of learning to trust Him with our emotional experience.

Sometimes God allows the quiet, so that we can finally hear what our hearts have been trying to tell us all along. Our conscious mind gets skilled at burying our deepest fears and feelings, but in the stillness, truth has space to surface.

I've come to realize that His light shines brightest, when I dare to visit the dark emotional places in my soul. God's heart as our Father is never to shame us in our emotional darkness, but to meet us there with His light and love. Like a tender father who enters his child's room during a nightmare, He comes not to condemn our fear but to comfort it, not to judge our sadness but to heal it.

St. John of the Cross spoke of the Dark Night of the Soul—those long, dry seasons when God feels emotionally distant. But in those nights, the soul learns to trust God's love beyond feelings, to know whose we are, even when we can't feel His presence.

His silence isn't abandonment—it's His patient, loving presence giving us space to be honest about what's really going on in our hearts without the pressure to "feel better" right away.

Listening as Transformation

In John 8, Jesus was put in a difficult situation when the Pharisees brought a woman caught in adultery to Him. Instead of reacting, He knelt and wrote in the sand. He listened—not just to their accusations but to the heart of the moment. He responded with grace and truth.

To listen is not simply to hear sounds. It is to create space for the soul of another person to emerge. Listening is soul care. It's a holy invitation to become present—not only to others, but to ourselves and to the voice of God.

Jesus first listened to the scribes and Pharisees as they brought their accusation against the woman caught in adultery. He didn't interrupt or cut them short. He allowed them to be heard—so that their words could become a mirror, not just for others, but for themselves.

Just as Jesus listened to the Pharisees, so too He listens when we make accusations—about others, or even about ourselves. He doesn't rush to condemn or correct. He listens. He gives space. And then, when we are finished speaking, He invites us to pay attention to what the voice of grace has to say.

He said gently: "Neither do I condemn thee: go, and sin no more" (John 8:11).

This is the posture of Jesus—always listening, always gracious, always leading us toward healing, not shame. God's heart as our Father is revealed in Jesus' response—patient listening, followed by grace-filled truth that sets us free rather than binds us in condemnation.

As we develop the discipline of listening, we begin to notice which voice is leading within us. When we're rushing through life, rarely pausing to listen, we often react from wounds, perform for approval, or hide behind masks. But in the practice of deep listening, our truest self emerges—the part of us that is secure in God's love and naturally responds with His character. Through listening, we slowly learn to live from our truest identity in Christ, rather than from the false versions of ourselves that the world has shaped.

Listening creates the sacred space where transformation happens. It's in the pause between stimulus and response that we can choose which self leads—the wounded one or the healed one, the performing one or the authentic one.

Final Reflection

So here we are at the end of our first step in answering "Who am Eye!" And perhaps you're discovering what I've learned: the answer doesn't come from looking inward harder at yourself, but from learning to listen more deeply to the One who made you.

Wholeness is not the absence of pain—it's the presence of Christ in all our pain. God's heart as our Father is to be present with us in every season—the joyful ones and the painful ones. He doesn't promise to remove all suffering, but He promises to be Emmanuel, God with us, in the midst of it all.

Think about Samuel for a moment. He didn't discover his calling by trying harder to be a prophet. He discovered it by learning to recognize the voice that had been calling his name all along. In the same way, your identity isn't something you achieve—it's something you receive as you learn to listen to the Father who has known you since before you were born.

As you sit with these questions, listen not just with your mind, but with your heart. Let the Holy Spirit whisper to you about who you really are in God's eyes:

Final Reflection Questions

Before we move forward, consider these questions:

1. **Which voices from your past still compete with God's voice about who you are?**

2. **When have you felt most heard by God, and what was He telling you about your worth?**

3. **What would change, if you truly believed God's voice defines you more than any other voice?**

Summary: Discovering Who Am Eye and Whose Am Eye Through Listening

Through this chapter, you've discovered that:

Who Am Eye? is answered not by looking inward harder, but by listening to the One who made you. Like Samuel, you discover your calling and identity by learning to recognize God's voice calling your name. You are not defined by your performance or circumstances—you are defined by what your heavenly Father speaks over you.

Whose Am Eye? becomes clear as you learn to distinguish between competing voices. You belong to the God who calls you by name, who knows you intimately, and whose voice of love and truth defines your worth. When you remember whose you are, you find the courage to be honest about where you are.

The foundation of discovering your true identity starts here: learning to listen to the heart of the One who has known you since before you were born. As you tune your spiritual ears to His voice, you begin to hear the identity He's been speaking over you all along.

Call to Action

Practice 5 minutes of silence daily this week. Set aside time to simply listen without agenda.

Identify your "Listening Chair"—a specific place for quiet reflection and prayer.

Use "Tell me more" once each day with someone close to you, focusing on hearing their heart.

Ask God to reveal one area where your soul feels unheard, then practice bringing that honesty to Him.

Key Principle

The soul is the battleground where identity is won or lost. But when we surrender our wounded souls to the Master Healer, He doesn't just mend—He transforms them, helping us live more consistently from our truest identity rather than our coping mechanisms.

Scripture Foundation

Proverbs 27:6 | Romans 8:28 | Proverbs 4:23 | James 1:19 | Proverbs 28:13 | Psalm 139:14 | Lamentations 3:22 | 2 Chronicles 16:9 | Psalm 42:11 | 2 Corinthians 4:16 | Luke 4:18 | Psalm 23:3 | Psalm 119:114

Now that you've learned to feel your emotions without fear and understand which of the Four Selves might be activated by different feelings, you're ready to discover something crucial: the emotions you've been avoiding often show up most powerfully in your closest relationships. When we numb our own pain, we often lose the ability to truly connect with others' hearts too. But when we learn emotional courage through our relationship with God, it transforms how we love everyone around us—our family, friends, and community.

Chapter 2 will help you see how these patterns show up in your most important relationships. We'll discover how emotional honesty becomes the foundation for authentic connection and how your True Self transforms the way you love others.

Chapter 2

Body - Temple Of The Holy Spirit

"The body is not merely a shell for the soul and spirit, but a temple designed by God to house His presence. When surrendered to the Holy Spirit, our physical form becomes an instrument through which divine life flows into the world."

Watchman Nee

From Listening to Living

In Chapter 1, we learned to "listen to hear the heart"—to attune our ears not only to others, but to God's voice speaking over our identity. We discovered that transformation begins not with looking deeper into ourselves, but with learning to truly listen to the One who made us.

Now we move from hearing truth to embodying it. What I continue to discover and experience in my journey—what still fills me with wonder and excitement—is that it's not just our ears that need to be surrendered to God. Our entire physical being—this body—was designed to be His sacred dwelling place.

The more I discover about how God designed my body for love, service, and worship, the more amazed I become at His intricate purpose for every part of us. And I can tell you this with absolute certainty: the greatest peace that I know as a human being is when I am fully aware of the abiding physical presence of the Holy Spirit within me.

This unity with God's Spirit is what my entire person yearns for. It is this peace and complete feeling of love that compels me to want to praise His name—the name of Jesus, who gave His body on the cross to set me free.

This deep longing for connection with our Creator is something we all share as His children. You and I, we are brothers and sisters in Christ, members of the same body. As Paul reminds us: "For just as each of us has one body with many members, and these members do not all have the same function, so in Christ we, though many, form one body, and each member belongs to all the others" (Romans 12:4-5).

This understanding changes everything about how we see ourselves and each other—we're family, walking this journey together.

When we know whose we are—beloved children of the God who designed our physical form with intentional love—we can approach our bodies not with shame or neglect, but with the reverence due to His dwelling place.

Different Versions of Ourselves

Here's something I've noticed in my own life and in walking with others: depending on our spiritual condition and what life is throwing at us, different versions of ourselves seem to show up in how we treat our physical bodies.

Sometimes I find myself honoring my body as God's temple—eating well, resting appropriately, using my physical strength to serve others with joy. In these moments, I feel aligned with how God designed me to live.

Other times, I catch myself punishing my body through overwork, neglecting basic needs, or using my physical presence to prove my worth rather than simply being present with others. It's like a different version of me takes over—one driven by fear or performance rather than love.

And then there are times when I'm so focused on how my body appears to others—whether I look successful, healthy, or spiritual enough—that I lose sight of the fact that my body is meant to be an instrument of worship, not a tool for image management.

I've learned that recognizing these different patterns in how we relate to our physical selves is actually the beginning of transformation. Our bodies tell the story of which part of us is leading at any given moment.

Your Body: God's Divine Habitation

Here's a truth that transformed how I see my physical body: God places such incredible value on your physical body that He calls it His divine sanctuary. Scripture reminds us that you are not your own: "Or do you not know that your body is a temple of the Holy Spirit within you, whom you have from God? You are not your own, for you were bought with a price. So glorify God in your body" (1 Corinthians 6:19-20).

You were bought at a price that Heaven itself paid to set you free from the market of slavery. Yes, your body is no longer for sale in that marketplace. You are free to worship the One who set you free. This is an act of gratitude.

When I first experienced this liberating freedom, I was moved with such overwhelming gratitude that it overflowed into worship. This worship was audible—I couldn't contain the praise. My hands were raised in the air, my heart was beating with excitement, while my mind was completely at peace. There were tingling sensations that covered my skin from the crown of my head to the soles of my feet. My head was turned upward to the One who created those heavens and all the physical elements around me. I was in total surrender, and to this very day, I love surrendering my body in its entirety to the One who created me—the One who knows every cell, every atom in my body that is miraculously held together by laminin.

Let me share something that will astound you about God's intimate design. Laminin is a protein found throughout your entire body—it's literally what holds your cells together. Scientists have discovered that this essential protein, which exists in every living creature, naturally forms the shape of a cross. Think about this: Jesus Christ is not only "upholding the universe by the word of his power" Hebrews 1:3, but He's holding every single cell in your body together through proteins shaped like the very cross on which He died for you.

Every moment of your life, your physical being is sustained by millions of tiny crosses working within you. You are fearfully and wonderfully made, held together by His love in the most personal, distinctive, and miraculous way imaginable.

Your physical form wasn't created merely for survival or even pleasure—it was designed for worship, for intimacy with the Creator of the universe who literally holds you together from the inside out.

But this very body is also designed to be a vessel of service to others—this is how we physically express our love. We were commissioned to take these bodies and spread the gospel: "Go therefore and make disciples of all nations, baptizing them in the name of the Father and of the Son and of the Holy Spirit, teaching them to observe all that I have commanded you" (Matthew 28:19-20).

It all starts with the physical act of surrender to God, and then flows naturally into service to others.

Your hands become His hands to heal and comfort. Your feet become His feet to carry the good news. Your voice becomes His voice to speak truth and encouragement. Your very presence becomes a tangible expression of His love in this world.

When Fear Takes Control of Our Physical Expression

But there is another reality we must face: when we're operating from fear, insecurity, or unhealed wounds, our bodies often become instruments of something other than worship. Instead of expressing God's love, they can become tools for self-protection, performance, or control.

I've watched this happen in my own life during seasons of ministry stress. My body language would change—shoulders tense, jaw tight, movements hurried and agitated. Rather than being a calm presence that reflected God's peace, my physical presence was communicating anxiety and the need to control outcomes. People could feel the stress radiating from me before I even spoke.

Satan knows how precious your body is to God, and he works tirelessly to subtly tempt you to misuse it. The body forms such a crucial part of our human identity, and the enemy is fully aware of this. If he can manage to destroy, distort, or defile our relationship with our physical being, he has won a significant part of the identity battle.

This is why attacks on body image, physical health,

sexual purity, and bodily stewardship are so prevalent—Satan understands that when we see our bodies as enemies rather than gifts, we lose sight of whose we are.

Understanding this holy stewardship helps us recognize why Satan targets our physical senses with such intensity. Think about it with me: in Genesis chapter 3, how did Satan tempt Eve? Through her senses—what she saw, heard, and desired to taste. He used her God-given physical design against her, leading her into deception through sensory stimulation.

This same strategy continues today. Your five senses—what you see, hear, touch, taste, and smell—are often the first access points the enemy uses to distort your identity and separate you from God's truth.

The Body as Truth-Teller

Here's something fascinating I've discovered: our bodies often reveal which version of ourselves is in control before our minds even recognize it.

When I'm operating from my truest identity in Christ, my body naturally expresses peace, openness, and genuine presence. My voice is calm, my posture is relaxed but attentive, and people often comment that they feel safe around me.

But when I'm driven by the need to prove myself or manage others' perceptions, my body tells a different story. I talk faster, gesture more frantically, and occupy space in a way that demands attention rather than inviting connection.

And when I'm operating from old wounds or insecurities, my body instinctively moves into protective mode—arms crossed, avoiding eye contact, or positioning myself to be able to escape quickly if needed.

Our bodies are incredibly honest. They reveal what's really going on inside us, often before we're consciously aware of it ourselves. Learning to pay attention to what our physical selves are communicating, can become a powerful tool for recognizing when we need to realign with who God created us to be.

Understanding how our bodies reveal which version of ourselves is leading naturally, brings us to an important question: How do we reclaim our physical selves as instruments of worship rather than warfare?

Reclaiming Your Body as God's Instrument

Here's what I've learned through my own struggles and in walking with many believers: as we learn to live from the Spirit rather than the flesh, we can reclaim our physical body as a vessel of worship, not warfare.

I remember wrestling with this truth during a particularly difficult season in my ministry. I had been treating my body like an obstacle to spiritual growth, pushing through exhaustion, ignoring stress signals, believing that somehow denying my physical needs made me more spiritual. In those seasons when my body was exhausted, my soul felt depleted, even though I was working for the Lord. The sad thought is that my spirit also felt weighed down, and even though I was giving my all physically, it felt like I was giving nothing.

This is precisely why God says we are all members of the same body—we are not the entire body. I have mentored and coached and provided addiction counseling to several pastors over the years who, in some form or another, believed they had to carry the weight of everything alone. They physically gave up the race at some point because the human body wasn't designed to sustain that kind of burden.

But God showed many of those pastors and me that the body isn't the enemy of the soul—it's His chosen temple, designed to participate in the divine conversation He wants to have with His children. When we allow the Holy Spirit to guide us, even simple spiritual practices can reshape our default reactions and help us embody truth.

When we understand our physical design as God's beloved children, everything changes. Our bodies aren't obstacles to spiritual growth—they're essential partners in our journey of discovering whose we are. And that truth, my friend, can transform how you see yourself today.

While we learn to honor our bodies as God's temple today, we also carry a glorious hope that transforms how we view our current physical limitations and struggles.

Hope for Your Future Body

Now, let me share something that fills me with anticipation every time I think about it. Scripture teaches us that this physical body you inhabit right now—with all its aches, limitations, and struggles—will one day be completely transformed. As Paul explains in 1 Corinthians 15, at the resurrection your body will be raised imperishable, transformed into a spiritual body perfectly suited for eternity with God.

This truth gives me hope on my hardest days, and I pray it does the same for you. Paul calls it a mystery: "Behold! I tell you a mystery. We shall not all sleep, but we shall all be changed, in a moment, in the twinkling of an eye, at the last trumpet. For the trumpet will sound, and the dead will be raised imperishable, and we shall be changed" (1 Corinthians 15:51-52).

Can you imagine it? This miraculous transformation is part of your eternal promise.

When you understand that God has an amazing future

planned for your body—completely healed and perfected—it actually changes how you care for it right now. This hope doesn't make you neglect your body; it makes you treasure it even more. You can take good care of yourself, without worrying about every ache, limitation, or imperfection, because you know that who you really are, goes far beyond what your body can or can't do today.

Your Daily Practical Instrument of Righteousness

Now, let me speak directly to your heart about something that changed my life when I finally understood it. Your body is not neutral—it's either an instrument of righteousness or a vessel being misused by the enemy.

I want to caution you that this is a choice that only you can make, and it's one you'll face repeatedly. Every morning when you wake up—before you check your phone, before you worry about your schedule—you have the opportunity to surrender your eyes, your hands, your mouth, your heart to God's service. You can choose to use your physical strength for His glory, your senses for His truth, your very presence as an expression of His love.

I started doing this years ago, and it transformed not just my ministry, but my entire relationship with God. When I consciously offer my body to Him each morning, I'm acknowledging that I am His chosen vessel, and everything I do with this physical form matters to Him.

The choice becomes clearer when we recognize the different ways we can inhabit our bodies. We can live from fear, constantly trying to protect or prove ourselves. We can live from image management, carefully controlling how we appear to others. We can live from unfiltered honesty about our physical and spiritual condition. Or we can live from the deep security of knowing we are God's beloved, allowing our bodies to naturally express His character through us.

Your body is far more than flesh and bone—it is the very expression of your identity in Christ. As the temple of the Holy Spirit, it becomes the sacred space where worship flows from your heart, where healing power touches a broken world, where righteousness is lived out daily, and where grace is made tangible through your hands, your voice, your presence.

Summary: Your Body as God's Sacred Temple

Through this chapter, you've discovered that:

Who Am Eye? is expressed through how you treat and use your physical body. You are God's masterpiece, fearfully and wonderfully made, held together by His love at the cellular level. Your body tells the story of which version of yourself is leading—fear, performance, image management, or your True Self resting in His love.

Whose Am Eye? is declared through your body as God's temple. You belong to the One who designed every cell, who holds you together with cross-shaped proteins, who calls your physical form His dwelling place. When you remember whose you are, you can surrender your body as an instrument of righteousness rather than a tool for self-protection.

Your physical form is not an obstacle to spiritual growth—it's an essential partner in discovering whose you are and expressing that identity to the world.

Final Reflection

As we conclude our exploration of the body as God's temple, I want you to sit with these questions. Don't rush through them.

Let God speak to your heart as you consider each one:

1. **How does knowing you belong to God, change how you treat His temple—your body?**

2. **What is your body telling you about which version of yourself has been leading lately?**

3. **What would surrender look like in one specific area of your physical life this week?**

Call to Action

This week, practice these two specific steps:

Morning Surrender: Each morning, place your hands on your heart and pray: "Lord, this body is Your temple. Use it for Your glory today."

Body Awareness: Notice when stress, fear, or performance pressure shows up in your physical posture, and pause to realign with God's truth about whose you are.

Key Principle

God created your body not to be silenced by shame, but to be surrendered in love. When your body aligns with His truth, it becomes an instrument of praise that brings Him glory and brings you joy.

Scripture Foundation

1 Corinthians 6:19-20 | Genesis 1:27 | Romans 12:1 | Romans 6:13-14 | Galatians 5:16 | Matthew 28:19-20 | 1 Corinthians 15:51-52 | Romans 12:4-5 | Hebrews 1:3

As we move from understanding your body as God's temple to exploring how your soul processes life's experiences, remember that your physical being is the vessel through which your inner world expresses itself. In Chapter 3, we'll discover how your soul—the processing center of your thoughts, emotions, and will—works in harmony with your spirit-filled body to shape your identity and relationships with God and others. We'll also explore how different aspects of who you are emerge through your soul's processing, building on what we've begun to see about the various ways we can inhabit our physical lives.

Chapter 3

SOUL - THE PROCESSING CENTER

"The soul is like a container. At birth, a baby's soul is pure—unstained by toxic relationships, trauma, or sin. But as life unfolds, we encounter experiences that leave deep impressions on the soul."

Dr. Rob Reimer

Now We Get Personal: Diving Deep Below the Surface

In Chapter 2, we explored the body—what can be seen with the naked eye, touched with human hands, and observed by others. We discovered how our physical selves serve as the temple of the Holy Spirit and carry our stories outwardly for the world to see. We learned that our bodies are not obstacles to spiritual growth, but essential partners in our journey of discovering whose we are. We also started to observe how we express ourselves through our bodies—sometimes honoring God's temple, sometimes driven by fear or performance, sometimes focused on managing our image.

But now we get personal. Now we dive deep below the surface of what is visible to the naked eye. We're moving inward to the soul—that hidden, sacred space where your real story is stored. This is where nobody else can see, where you wrestle with your deepest questions, where your strongest emotions live, and where your identity is truly forged.

If the body is the house everyone sees from the street, the soul is where you actually live—behind closed doors, in the quiet moments, in the spaces between your public persona and your private reality. It's here, in the depths of the soul, where your most hidden wounds and your most precious hopes reside. And it's here where God does His most transformative work of identity restoration.

I've learned this truth personally through years of wrestling with fear and anxiety that no one could see from the outside. While my body appeared strong and my ministry seemed successful, my soul was processing deep questions about my worth and God's faithfulness that took years to fully understand. The crushing anxiety I felt during seasons of uncertainty—wondering if I was truly called to ministry, if God really saw me as His son—those battles were fought entirely in the hidden places of my soul.

It was when I experienced God's healing touch in those hidden places that I realized how much transformation was needed below the surface. The Greek word "Abba" that Jesus used, carries incredible significance in this context. In Jesus' time, Roman soldiers often had children by their slave wives, but these children were never considered legitimate members of the household—they had no inheritance, no family name, no place at the table. But when Jesus referred to His Father as "Abba"—the intimate term an adopted son would use—He was declaring something revolutionary: through His finished work on the cross, we are now full members of God's family through adoption. We have a name, an inheritance, and a permanent place at the Father's table.

When we understand that our souls belong to the God who created, redeems, and restores them, we can approach soul care not from shame or fear, but from the security of knowing we are souls being renewed by the Master Healer. Our souls are not beyond repair—they are being transformed by the One who specializes in making broken things beautiful.

It's also here where we begin to understand why those different versions of ourselves emerge. The soul is where we process life's experiences, and depending on what we've been through and how we've learned to cope, different patterns of thinking, feeling, and responding take shape.

The Soul as Your Processing Center

Think of your soul as mission control for your inner life. It's where your intellect processes thoughts, your will makes decisions, and your emotions respond to life's experiences.

Everything that happens to you—every conversation, every disappointment, every moment of joy—gets filtered through your soul's processing center. This is where the deepest battles of identity and spiritual transformation unfold.

Through our senses, thoughts are stimulated. What we think shapes what we do, and what we do influences how we feel. It's a beautiful, complex system that God designed to help us navigate life in wisdom and grace.

But here's what I've discovered in my own journey and

in pastoring others: this system can be hijacked. And when it is, different ways of being in the world emerge—different versions of ourselves that we learned to rely on for survival, acceptance, or self-protection.

Remember Genesis 3? Satan didn't attack Eve's body first—he went straight for her soul. He twisted God's words, contradicted His truth, and planted seeds of doubt about God's character and her own identity. When Eve and Adam disobeyed, their perception of themselves and God changed dramatically. They became afraid, ashamed, and defensive. I believe this was the moment their souls were traumatized by the knowledge of evil, and they began to hide, blame, and distort reality—patterns we still struggle with today.

This is where our different ways of being in the world often originate—in the soul's attempt to process pain and protect us from further harm.

The truth I've had to learn the hard way: pain entered the human experience, and God still gives us a choice—to embrace our pain and learn from it, or to avoid it and stay stuck. As I often tell people I pastor, "No pain, no gain" isn't just a workout motto. It's a spiritual principle.

Think about it—we enter this world through pain. The agony of labor, the intense pressure of birth, the sharp intake of that first breath. But oh, the joy that floods a mother's heart when she finally holds her baby in her arms! The pain was the pathway to the miracle.

It's the same with metamorphosis. The process of a caterpillar becoming a butterfly involves what scientists call "imaginal discs"—the creature literally dissolves in the cocoon, its old form dying completely before the new emerges. It's painful, messy, and seemingly destructive. But when that butterfly finally takes flight for the first time, spreading wings that were impossible in its former state, the beauty and freedom make every moment of the transformation worth it.

No pain—no children. No pain—no harvest. No pain—no new creation. Friend, I've discovered that pain can be our tutor, not our tyrant, if we let it lead us to the truth of who we are becoming.

How Our Souls Reveal the Four Selves

As I've walked with people through their healing journeys, I've noticed four distinct patterns that tend to emerge, depending on where someone is spiritually and what life has taught them about survival and love:

Sometimes our souls process life with raw honesty about both the beauty and the brokenness we're experiencing. In these moments, we're real about our struggles without being controlled by them, honest about our joys without being naive about the world's pain. This feels like the most authentic version of ourselves.

Sometimes our souls get hijacked by old wounds and fears, causing us to react from places of self-protection, performance, or control. We might become people-pleasers desperate for approval, workaholics trying to prove our worth, or controllers attempting to create safety through manipulation. This version feels driven and exhausting.

Sometimes our souls carefully curate what we allow others to see, editing our responses and managing our image because vulnerability feels too risky. We become skilled at saying what people want to hear: hiding the parts of our story that feel too messy or complicated. This version feels safe but lonely.

And sometimes—in our best moments—our souls process life from a place of deep security in God's love. We respond rather than react, love without needing something back, and naturally express God's character through our unique personality. This version feels like coming home to who we really are.

Understanding these different ways our soul can process life helps us recognize why we at times feel like strangers to ourselves, and why transformation can feel so challenging.

The Soul's Control Tower: Three Essential Systems

Your soul processes life through three interconnected faculties, like an air traffic control tower managing incoming flights:

Intellect (Radar System) — gathering and processing information

Will (Flight Controller) — making decisions about what gets permission to "land"

Emotions (Weather System) — affecting how everything feels and flows

When your control tower is functioning well, you experience peace, clear thinking, and wise decisions. But when there's interference, storms, or poor communication between systems, chaos can result—and this is often when the different versions of ourselves take over.

Intellect: Your Soul's Radar System

Your mind is more than just a thinking machine—it's like the radar system in that air traffic control tower, constantly gathering and processing information about your identity. Our thoughts are stimulated through sensory experiences—what we see, hear, touch, smell, and taste all send signals to our soul's radar system.

The thoughts we repeatedly think, become the beliefs we hold about ourselves. Those beliefs become the lens through which we see everything. This is where the spiritual battle for identity is most intense.

But here's where it gets complex: depending on our past experiences, our radar system can become calibrated to detect different kinds of threats or opportunities. If we were raised in an environment where love was conditional on performance, our radar becomes hypervigilant about any signs of disapproval. If we experienced abandonment, our radar constantly scans for signs that people are pulling away.

These different calibrations create different ways of processing information, which lead to different versions of ourselves showing up in response.

When trauma hijacks the radar system, it becomes overactive and unreliable. It starts giving the flight controller false readings, detecting threats that may not actually exist. This causes overreaction in the control tower—every blip on the screen looks like danger.

This is often when our wounded, self-protective version takes over. We might become defensive before anyone attacks, suspicious when people are actually trying to help, or controlling when surrender would actually bring more peace.

Eventually, this false state of mind causes us to doubt our own judgment, our competence, our very ability to discern truth from lies. The very system designed to help us navigate life safely becomes the source of our greatest insecurity.

Finding Truth in God's Radar Manual

When our soul's radar system gets hijacked by trauma or pain, we need to recalibrate it with God's truth. This is exactly what happened to me during a particularly challenging season in ministry, when criticism from some church members sent my soul into a tailspin. My young pastoral heart couldn't process the complexity of leading people through difficulty, so the harsh words became evidence that I was failing as a leader. That thought, rehearsed over weeks, became a belief that shaped months of self-doubt and ministry insecurity.

What I learned later is what Heifetz teaches: leadership isn't about having all the answers, but about helping others adapt to challenges. To lead from your True Self is to lead from conviction—not comfort.

Paul's teaching in Romans 12:2 helped me search for the truth about what was going on in my radar system: "And be not fashioned according to this world: but be ye transformed by the renewing of your mind, and ye may prove what is the good and acceptable and perfect will of God".

I had to reference God's radar manual—His Word—to find the truth about how my radar system was supposed to function.

In the process, I discovered something life-changing: I was not alone in the control tower. Captain Holy Spirit was right there to calm the storm that existed in my soul. He said, "You're doing fine. Follow my guidance and all will work out well."

When we feed our minds on His Word, we begin to think His thoughts about us, and those thoughts transform our identity—and help us live more consistently from our truest self, rather than our wounded or defensive versions.

Will: Your Soul's Flight Controller

Your will is like the flight controller in that tower—it's where you make the critical decisions about which thoughts get permission to "land" in your heart and which ones need to be redirected. Your intellect may know the truth about who you are in Christ, but your will determines which thoughts get to land.

Here's how the will shapes which version of ourselves show

up: our daily choices build our character, and our character expresses our identity. Every choice either reinforces our truest identity or strengthens a wounded or false version:

- When you choose forgiveness over bitterness, you strengthen the version of yourself that lives as a forgiven person

- When you choose vulnerability over image management, you reinforce the authentic version of yourself

- When you choose courage over fear, you strengthen your identity as God's beloved

- When you choose performance over rest, you reinforce the version that believes love must be earned

Your will is the bridge between knowing who you are and living like it. This is where the rubber meets the road in soul transformation.

Emotions: Your Soul's Weather System

Your emotions are like the weather conditions surrounding that control tower—they affect how everything feels and flows, but they don't determine the flight plan. They reveal what you truly believe about yourself and your circumstances, and they often signal which version of yourself is in the driver's seat.

Your emotional patterns often expose the lies you've believed about yourself and the areas where God's truth hasn't yet taken root:

- If you believe "I'm not lovable," you'll feel anxious when people get close (wounded version leading)

- If you believe "I must be perfect," you'll feel exhausted trying to manage every outcome (performing version leading)
- If you believe "I'm God's beloved," you'll feel peace even in difficult circumstances (truest version leading)
- If you believe "People will reject the real me," you'll feel lonely even in crowds (hidden version leading)

Remember this truth: You are not your emotions, and you are not defined by which version of yourself shows up on any given day. Your emotions are messengers, but your identity is anchored in Christ's truth, not in your feelings or your patterns.

Understanding Your Emotions: Data, Not Directives

One of the most liberating truths I can share with you is this: Your emotions are data, not directives.

Let me explain what I mean. Your emotions provide valuable information about what's happening in your soul and which version of yourself might be taking over, but they shouldn't automatically drive your decisions or actions. When you feel angry, that anger is telling you something important—perhaps a boundary has been crossed or an injustice has occurred. But the emotion itself doesn't tell you how to respond.

Here's how emotions serve as helpful data about which version of yourself is emerging:

- Reactive anger might signal your wounded self is trying to protect you

- Performance anxiety might indicate your people-pleasing self is taking over

- Shame-based hiding might reveal your self-protective self is in control

- Peace in difficulty might show your truest self is leading from God's security

But when emotions become our boss, they can steer us in the wrong direction. Instead of helping us return to our truest self, they end up reinforcing whichever wounded or defensive part of us is already in charge.

I learned these lessons painfully through years of letting anxiety control my decision-making in ministry. Whenever I felt overwhelmed by the demands of pastoral care, my emotions would scream, "You can't handle this! You're going to fail!" But those emotional directives nearly caused me to abandon the very calling God had placed on my life. Over the years I have learned to pause, listen to what my emotions were telling me about my own limitations and need for God's strength, and then let God's Word guide my response.

The goal isn't to ignore our emotions—it's to develop emotional intelligence guided by spiritual wisdom. We acknowledge what our emotions are telling us about which version of ourselves is showing up, but we let God's Word and the Holy Spirit guide our response back to who we really are in Him. This is what James meant when he wrote: "Ye know this, my beloved brethren. But let every man be swift to hear, slow to speak, slow to wrath" (James 1:19).

The Soul as God's Container: Personal Restoration

Understanding how wounds contaminate our soul's processing helps us appreciate the beauty of God's restoration work. Dr. Rob Reimer teaches a beautiful truth: the soul functions like a container designed to hold God's love and truth. At birth, our soul is pure—unstained by toxic relationships, trauma, or sin. But as life unfolds, we encounter experiences that leave deep impressions.

These experiences often shape which versions of ourselves we learn to rely on. When the container is damaged through pain, betrayal, or trauma, different coping mechanisms develop—some healthy, some not. We might learn to hide our true selves to avoid rejection, perform to earn love, or become defensive to prevent further hurt.

When I struggled with anxiety and fear during my early ministry years, it didn't just create worry—it contaminated my soul's purity with lies about my competence and God's faithfulness. As a young pastor, I tried to fill my container with people's approval and ministerial success, thinking achievement would prove my calling. But these substitutes only strengthened the performing, image-managing version of myself rather than helping me rest in who I already was in Christ.

The beautiful truth is that God specializes in soul restoration. He doesn't just patch up the cracks—He replaces what was broken with something stronger, helping us live more consistently from our truest identity rather than our coping mechanisms.

I personally experienced how the blood of Christ covered my container on the inside. Where there were holes, they were completely covered. My soul is no longer leaking empty. The abiding presence of the Holy Spirit now fills me with God's joy and peace, and the desperate need for people's approval and ministerial performance no longer drives my identity. What once felt essential for survival became unnecessary when I discovered my true worth in Christ.

Soul Healing: God's Specialty

I've discovered that the soul is where spiritual warfare often manifests most intensely, but it's also where I've experienced God's healing power most profoundly. The enemy aims to strengthen the wounded, false versions of us, by feeding our souls lies about our identity and God's character.

However, in Christ, we have authority to stand against these lies and choose to live from our truest identity. Jesus declared in Luke 4:18: "The Spirit of the Lord is upon me, because he anointed me to preach good tidings to the poor: He hath sent me to proclaim release to the captives, And recovering of sight to the blind, To set at liberty them that are bruised" (Luke 4:18).

Soul healing happens when we:

- Bring our wounds into the light of God's truth
- Recognize which versions of the self developed as coping mechanisms
- Renounce the lies we've believed about ourselves
- Receive God's love in the broken places
- Forgive those who hurt us (and ourselves)
- Choose to live from our truest identity rather than our protective patterns

The goal isn't a perfect soul—it's a surrendered one that increasingly expresses who we really are in Christ.

Summary: Your Soul as God's Processing Center

Through this chapter, you've discovered that:

Who Am Eye? is forged in the soul's processing center where your intellect, will, and emotions work together. Different versions of yourself emerge based on how your soul has learned to process pain, joy, and life experiences. Your truest identity is discovered not by perfecting your soul's processing, but by surrendering it to the Master Healer who specializes in transformation.

Whose Am Eye? becomes clear as you understand that your soul belongs to the God who created it pure, who redeems it when damaged, and who restores it through His perfect love. You are not owned by your wounds, your coping mechanisms, or your emotional patterns—you belong to the One who sees your soul's true condition and loves you completely.

Your soul is not your master—it's your mission control center that works best when surrendered to the Captain who knows how to navigate every storm.

Final Reflection

Before we move forward, let me ask you some honest questions:

1. **When you feel anxious, angry, or overwhelmed, do you typically hide, perform, or fight back?**

2. **What painful experience is your soul still processing that affects how you see yourself today?**

3. **What would change if you surrendered the fighting, performance and hiding to God, instead of trying to manage them yourself?**

Call to Action

This week, practice these two essential steps:

Soul Awareness: When strong emotions arise, pause and ask: "What is this emotion telling me about which part of myself is leading right now?" before reacting.

Healing Prayer: Ask God to reveal one specific area where your soul needs His healing touch, then invite Him into that place with honesty and trust.

Key Principle

The soul is the battleground where identity is won or lost. But when we surrender our wounded souls to the Master Healer, He doesn't just mend—He transforms them, helping us live more consistently from our truest identity rather than our coping mechanisms.

Scripture Foundation

Genesis 1:26-27 | Romans 12:2 | Proverbs 4:23 | James 1:19 | Proverbs 27:19 | Psalm 139:14 | Lamentations 3:22 | 2 Chronicles 16:9 | Psalm 42:11 | 2 Corinthians 4:16 | Luke 4:18 | Psalm 23:3 | Psalm 119:114

As we move from understanding the soul as our processing center, to exploring the spirit as our communion with the divine, remember that if the soul is where our different patterns and coping mechanisms develop, the spirit is where God's truth about who we really are remains constant and secure. In Chapter 4, we'll discover how our spirit—that sacred dimension created for direct communion with God—anchors our truest identity in eternal truth that transcends every circumstance we face, and every version of ourselves that life's experiences have created.

> If the soul is where our stories are stored, the spirit is where God's story about us is written. It's time to discover what He's been saying about you all along.

Chapter 4

SPIRIT - COMMUNION WITH GOD

"The spirit is the noblest part of man and occupies the innermost area of his being. The spirit is capable of knowing and communicating with God. It is through the spirit that man touches the spiritual realm."

—Watchman Nee

From Soul Processing to Spirit Communion

In Chapter 3, we explored the soul—your processing center where intellect, will, and emotions work together to make sense of life's experiences. We discovered how different versions of ourselves emerge based on how our souls process life's experiences, especially pain and trauma. We saw how childhood wounds can hijack your soul's control tower, creating patterns that feel protective, but often leave us feeling like strangers to ourselves.

But we also learned that God specializes in soul restoration, transforming our wounded processing center into a place where His truth can take root and flourish.

Now we move even deeper, to the spirit—the part of your being created for direct communion with God and destined to live with Him eternally. Just like a ship is made to rest in the ocean, your spirit was designed to find its rest in God. If the soul asks, "Which version of myself is showing up today?" the spirit declares, "Whose love am I anchored in, no matter which winds are currently pushing my sails?"

Here's what completely revolutionized my understanding of identity: While the soul processes our human experiences and develops different coping patterns, the spirit is where God imparts His divine life. The soul can be wounded and need healing, but the spirit of a believer is already perfect, complete, and eternally secure in Christ.

This means that no matter which version of yourself shows up on any given day—whether you're struggling, performing, hiding, or thriving—your deepest identity remains unshaken. Your spirit is the anchor that holds steady while your soul learns to process life from truth rather than fear.

Your True Self Lives Here

For years, I exhausted myself trying to fix my spirit, make it more holy, more acceptable to God. I was running on empty from spiritual performance, constantly trying to strengthen the "right" version of myself while eliminating the "wrong" ones. Then I discovered something that changed my life: my spirit was already complete in Christ.

The question wasn't how to improve my spirit, but how to live from the security and wholeness I already possessed.

This understanding deepens what we begin to explore about the fundamental difference between asking "Who am I?"

and anchoring ourselves in "Whose am I?" When your spirit is your foundation, you discover that your identity flows from relationship with God rather than from your performance, circumstances, or even your soul's current processing patterns.

When we know whose we are—children of the eternal God—we can approach our spiritual life not from striving but from rest, not from fear but from the security of being perfectly loved.

Your Spirit: God's Inner Sanctuary

Let me share how I personally discovered this truth about the spirit's role in our identity. For the longest time, it was difficult for me to truly believe that my spirit could be the inner sanctuary of the Holy Spirit. Because of my past sins, I didn't feel worthy of such a holy God. Inside my spirit, I didn't have peace—instead, I yearned for a peace that I didn't even know was possible.

Have you ever walked into a sanctuary and immediately felt the calm, peace, love, and harmony that flows from God's presence? I used to experience that in church buildings but wondered why I couldn't find that same peace within myself.

But there came a defining day in my life—inside my own supermarket, when a drug lord's gang was waiting outside to end my life. Earlier that morning during my prayer time, I audibly heard the Lord say, "If you choose business, you are going to die. If you choose Me, I will give you life."

That day I surrendered it all to Jesus. It was in that moment, falling on my knees in my own store and crying out "I surrender it all," that I experienced the presence of the Holy Spirit for the first time in a completely different way. This time I wasn't experiencing His presence from the outside, coming at me from a church building or through someone else's prayer. This time it came from within—from the very core of my being.

This is where I discovered something profound: regardless of which version of myself had been running the show—the fearful businessman trying to control outcomes, the people-pleaser desperate for approval, the performer working to prove his worth—underneath all of that was my True Self, already complete and perfectly loved in Christ.

We all have these different versions of ourselves: fearful of failure, needing to control outcomes, at times people-pleasing and striving to perform. These all stem from the unrealistic expectations that society has placed on us—to fit in, to be socially accepted by our tribe.

Over the years, as I've continued to experience His presence, this reality has gradually shifted from doubt to deep belief. I've come to understand that my spirit truly is His place to dwell, to belong, to call His sanctuary of peace. And this truth remains constant whether I'm having a good day or a terrible one, whether I'm flowing in my gifts or struggling with my weaknesses.

Scripture describes this amazing truth: "Know ye not that ye are the temple of God, and that the Spirit of God dwelleth in you?" (1 Corinthians 3:16).

This understanding completely transformed how I approach the different versions of myself that show up. Instead of trying to eliminate the wounded or performing parts, I learned to live from the security of my spirit's union with God, allowing that foundation to gradually transform how my soul processes life.

Your Spirit: The Anchor That Keeps You Steady

Think of your spirit as an anchor that keeps you steady in God's love. While your soul (like a ship) may get tossed by circumstances, emotions, or reactions, your spirit remains anchored in the unshakeable truth of whose you are.

Your True Self lives in this anchored place—secure in Christ's love regardless of which version of yourself is currently showing up on the surface.

Just as we cannot create the ocean, we cannot create God's love—it simply is, vast and endless, surrounding us completely. Whether our ship is sailing smoothly or struggling through storms, whether we're drifting or navigating purposefully, we are always held by this infinite ocean of divine love.

Scripture reminds us of this unchanging reality: "For I am persuaded, that neither death, nor life, nor angels, nor principalities, nor powers, nor things present, nor things to come, Nor height, nor depth, nor any other creature, shall be able to separate us from the love of God, which is in Christ Jesus our Lord" (Romans 8:38-39).

Your spirit-anchor isn't just floating somewhere in the water—it's secured deep in the ocean floor of God's eternal love. This means that no matter how fierce the storms above, no matter how your ship gets tossed by waves of criticism, currents of comparison, or winds of circumstance, your anchor holds firm because it's embedded in something that cannot be moved or changed.

Three Sacred Functions: How Your Anchor Actually Works

Your spirit operates through three key functions that keep you connected to God's truth:

Intuition: Your Anchor's Weight

Just as an anchor's weight pulls it down toward the ocean floor, your spiritual intuition is constantly drawing you toward truth, always seeking the solid ground of God's reality. This isn't intellect—it's a knowing that transcends reasoning, a divine pull toward what is right, safe, and aligned with God's heart.

Even when your ship is being tossed by emotions or confused by circumstances, your spiritual intuition creates a downward pull toward truth. Like an anchor naturally sinking toward the bottom, your spirit naturally gravitates toward God's perspective, even when other versions of yourself are temporarily steering the ship.

Let me give you a real-life example from my own journey. There were seasons when I was caught up in trying to please everyone and prove my worth through what I did. During those times, whenever I said yes to things that weren't really what God wanted for me—maybe taking on extra commitments to look spiritual, or agreeing to projects just to avoid disappointing people—I'd feel this nagging uneasiness inside. It wasn't just guilt about being busy. It was something deeper.

My spirit knew I was off track and kept pulling me back toward what was true and right, even when my emotions were too messed up to think clearly about it.

Conscience: Your Anchor's Chain

The chain connects the ship to the anchor, providing the vital link between your daily life and your spiritual foundation. Your conscience works exactly like this—it's the connection that provides tension when you start drifting too far from your spiritual mooring.

Just as a ship's captain can feel the tug of the anchor chain when the vessel begins to drift, your conscience creates that moral tension when you begin moving away from who you really are in Christ. It's not condemnation—it's the gentle but firm pull that says, "You're drifting. Time to return to your foundation."

As I discovered while writing this book, the cherubim and the Ark of the Covenant provide a beautiful picture of how conscience works. The cherubim were crafted as one piece with the mercy seat, their wings overshadowing the very place where God's presence dwelled.

Your conscience operates from your True Self, calling you back to who you really are no matter which version of yourself is currently expressed. When your wounded self wants to retaliate, your conscience whispers mercy. When your performing self wants to take credit, your conscience points toward humility. When your hidden self wants to stay isolated, your conscience encourages authentic connection.

Moral DNA: Your Anchor's Flukes

Just as an anchor's flukes are specifically shaped to grip the ocean floor, your moral DNA is woven into the very fabric of your spirit with God's own character patterns. This divine imprint cannot be altered by circumstances, damaged by trauma, or destroyed by sin.

Here's what this means for your daily life:

- You were designed for righteousness—sin feels unnatural because it contradicts your spiritual DNA, even when you're operating from wounded places

- You hunger for truth—deception creates internal conflict because lies oppose your nature, even when you're tempted to hide or perform

- You long for authentic relationships—manipulation feels foreign to your True Self, even when fear drives you toward self-protection

I've seen this play out countless times in my own life. When I'm not living according to my true nature in Christ, there's this internal tension that won't go away. It's not condemnation—it's my moral DNA calling me back home to who I really am, regardless of which version of myself is currently struggling.

Your True Self: The Foundation in the Ocean Floor

When storms of criticism come, when currents of comparison try to pull you off course, when winds of circumstance threaten to drive you toward reactive patterns, your spirit-anchor holds you secure in the truth of whose you are. You might feel the ship swaying—your emotions might be chaotic, your thoughts confused—but your anchor keeps you from drifting into identity crisis because nothing can separate you from the love of God.

The moment you were saved, God breathed His life into your spirit. You became a new creation. Your spirit was instantly regenerated, made perfect, and eternally secure. This means:

Your True Self is already complete. It's not something you achieve through spiritual discipline or emotional healing—it's something you live from.

Your True Self remains constant. Whether you're struggling, thriving, hiding, or performing, your deepest identity in Christ doesn't change—like the ocean floor that remains steady regardless of the storms above.

Your True Self is the source. The goal isn't to eliminate other versions of yourself but to live from this foundation, allowing it to gradually transform how your soul processes life.

But when you're anchored in your True Self through your spirit's union with God, you can watch the sun set peacefully, knowing that the same God who controls its orbit also holds your life in His perfect hands. You can rest in the ocean of His love, trusting that even when you temporarily drift in other compass directions, you remain held by the One whose love never changes.

The goal isn't to eliminate the other compass directions. It's to learn to navigate from the security of being anchored in God's unchanging love. This means allowing True North to guide your course while extending grace to yourself when you temporarily drift in other directions

Living From Your Spirit vs. For Your Spirit

This distinction completely revolutionized my spiritual life and my understanding of the Four Selves that show up. For years, I lived for my spirit—constantly trying to prove my worth to God through ministry performance, spiritual disciplines, and religious activities. I was trying to strengthen my "spiritual" version while eliminating my "fleshly" versions.

Then I discovered the freedom of living from my spirit—from the security of who I already was in Christ. Friend, the difference is life-changing:

Living for your spirit says:

- "I must eliminate my struggling-wounded versions"
- "I need to perform spiritually to maintain God's love"
- "My identity depends on which version of myself shows up"

Living from your spirit says:

- "My True Self is secure regardless of my current struggles"
- "I operate from my identity as God's beloved child"
- "My actions flow from love, not from fear of being the 'wrong' version"

When I finally learned to live from my spirit instead of for my spirit, ministry became joy instead of burden. My relationship with God became rest instead of striving. I could acknowledge my wounded or performing parts, without being defined by them, because my foundation was secure.

Most importantly, I discovered that living from my True Self doesn't mean I never have difficult emotions or reactive patterns. It means I have a foundation that remains steady while my soul learns to process life from truth rather than fear.

How Your True Self Transforms All Versions

Here's something beautiful I've discovered: when you learn to live from your True Self—that secure, Spirit-anchored identity—it doesn't eliminate the other versions of yourself. Instead, it gradually transforms them.

Scripture captures this transformation perfectly: "Lie not one to another; seeing that ye have put off the old man with his doings, and have put on the new man, that is being renewed unto knowledge after the image of him that created him" (Colossians 3:9-10).

And again: "But we all, with unveiled face beholding as in a mirror the glory of the Lord, are transformed into the same image from glory to glory, even as from the Lord the Spirit" (2 Corinthians 3:18).

This progressive transformation is God's work in us: "Being confident of this very thing, that he who began a good work in you will perfect it until the day of Jesus Christ" (Philippians 1:6).

We become "new creatures" through Christ: "Wherefore if any man is in Christ, he is a new creature: the old things are passed away; behold, they are become new" (2 Corinthians 5:17).

The Spirit accomplishes this renewal from within: "But when the kindness of God our Saviour, and his love toward man, appeared, not by works done in righteousness, which we did ourselves, but according to his mercy he saved us, through the washing of regeneration and renewing of the Holy Spirit" (Titus 3:4-5).

Your honest, struggling self becomes a place of authentic connection with God and others, rather than shame or self-condemnation.

Your wounded, reactive self finds healing as it learns to process pain from the security of being loved, rather than from the fear of being abandoned.

Your performing, image-managing self relaxes into authenticity as it discovers that love doesn't have to be earned.

And your True Self becomes not just a spiritual concept but a lived reality—the natural expression of who you are when you're resting in God's love rather than striving for it.

Summary: Your Spirit as God's Anchor

Through this chapter, you've discovered that:

Who Am Eye? is anchored in God's Spirit—where your true self is anchored in the love of Christ. Your True Self lives here, already complete and perfect in Christ. This isn't another version you work to access—it's the foundation from which all transformation flows. Your identity doesn't depend on which version shows up—it's secure in your spirit's union with God.

Whose Am Eye? is settled forever in your spirit's connection to the eternal God. You belong to the One whose love surrounds you like an endless ocean, whose truth anchors you deeper than any storm can reach. Your spirit-anchor holds firm in the ocean floor of His unchanging character, ensuring you can never drift beyond His love.

Your spirit is the dimension of your being that was made to relate to God, and to be sustained and directed by God. When you live from your spirit, you live from your truest identity.

Final Reflection

As we conclude this exploration of the spirit, let me ask you some personal questions:

1. When do you feel most like your authentic self in God's presence?
2. What would change if you believed your spirit was already perfect and complete in Christ?
3. What would it look like to live from spiritual security rather than trying to earn God's approval?

Call to Action

This week, practice these two transformative steps:

Daily Spirit Connection: Start each morning by acknowledging that your True Self is already complete in Christ—you're not working for His love, you're working from it.

Anchor Awareness: When you feel reactive or defensive,

pause and remember that your identity is anchored deeper than any current storm—you belong to the God, whose love never changes.

Key Principle

Your spirit is the dimension of your being that was made to relate to God and to be sustained and directed by God. When you live from your spirit, you live from your truest identity—the foundation that transforms all other versions of yourself through love rather than elimination.

Scripture Foundation

Genesis 2:7 | Genesis 1:27 | John 1:12 | Ephesians 1:3 | Jeremiah 1:5 | 1 Corinthians 2:11 | 2 Corinthians 2:12 | Romans 8:38-39 | Hebrews 4:12 | Ecclesiastes 3:11 | Jeremiah 31:33 | 2 Corinthians 4:7 | 2 Corinthians 4:3 | Exodus 25:18,22 | Exodus 37:9 | 1 Corinthians 3:16 | Colossians 3:9-10 | 2 Corinthians 3:18 | Philippians 1:6 | 2 Corinthians 5:17 • Titus 3:4-5

Now that we understand how your spirit anchors your True Self in Christ's unchanging love, you're ready to see how this spiritual foundation translates into daily life. In Chapter 5, we'll explore a practical framework for recognizing and responding to the different aspects of yourself that show up moment by moment. You'll discover how to live more consistently from your True Self, while extending grace to all the other parts of your humanity that God is patiently transforming.

Chapter 5

The Four Selves - A Framework for Transformation

"The greatest issue facing the world today, with all its heartbreaking needs, is whether those who, by profession or culture, are identified as 'Christians' will become disciples – students, apprentices, practitioners – of Jesus Christ, steadily learning from him how to live the life of the Kingdom of the Heavens into every corner of human existence."

Dallas Willard

From Spiritual Foundation to Daily Reality

In the previous chapters, we've built a solid foundation: learning to listen to God's voice, honoring our bodies as His temple, understanding our soul's processing center, and discovering our spirit's communion with the divine. Now that you're anchored in whose you are, let's explore how this spiritual foundation translates into everyday life.

You might be wondering: "How do these three parts of me—body, soul, and spirit—actually work together when I'm trying to love my kids well, handle conflict at work, or figure out what God wants from me?"

Here's what I've discovered after years of wrestling with this question myself: depending on where you are spiritually and what life is throwing at you, different versions of yourself show up—and recognizing which version is leading can change everything about how you experience your days.

When we know whose we are—beloved children of the eternal God—we can approach our inner complexity not with shame but with grace, understanding that Christ is forming our True Self through every season and circumstance.

My Personal Discovery

Let me tell you about the moment I first realized that different versions of myself show up in different situations. It was during my early years in ministry when I found myself trapped in what I now call "the ministry perfectionism prison."

I believed a lie that controlled many aspects of my pastoral life: "You cannot afford to make mistakes." Every sermon had to be flawless, every counseling session had to produce breakthrough, every leadership decision had to be exactly right.

What I discovered was that different selves would emerge depending on the specific ministry challenges I faced. When things were going smoothly, my Actual Self and True Self could lead naturally from a place of rest in God's love. But when challenging situations arose that triggered childhood wounds, other selves would surface.

The breakthrough came during a particularly difficult

season when I had made a significant mistake in handling a church conflict. I was drowning in shame and self-condemnation when God whispered this truth to my heart: "Your mistakes don't disqualify you from My love—they reveal places where My grace wants to go deeper."

This was when I first understood what I now call the Four Selves—and more importantly, I learned that living from my True Self wasn't about becoming perfect, but about resting in His perfect love for me.

I realized the very ministerial imperfections I feared, were opportunities for His grace to shine through. My pastoral mistakes weren't disqualifications—they were doorways for others to see that God uses imperfect leaders to do beautiful things.

This was when I discovered the peace of working WITH the Holy Spirit instead of FOR Him. In many of my sermons, I now preach that God is teaching me to work FROM my rest, not FOR my rest. The anxiety melted away when I realized He was in control and I didn't need to control anything. I could relax in His presence rather than work for it.

That's when I first understood what I now call the Four Selves—and more importantly, I learned that living from my True Self wasn't about becoming perfect, but about resting in His perfect love for me.

This is why I've learned to be grateful for difficult ministry moments. They don't disqualify me—they reveal where God wants to do His deepest work of identity formation.

Sadly, we live in a society—and often attend churches—that have cultivated a culture of shaming people for their mistakes rather than creating safe spaces for growth and healing. This culture feeds into something much deeper and more spiritually destructive: it drives us toward secrecy and constant image management instead of the authentic community God designed us for.

When we fear that our struggles will be met with judgment rather than grace, we learn to hide our Actual Self and present only the versions of ourselves that we think will be accepted. The very places that should be sanctuaries for broken people to find healing become performance stages where we're terrified to be real.

God has placed this message of sanctification on my heart. This is why understanding the Four Selves becomes so crucial—not just for personal growth, but for creating the kind of communities where people can be honest about which self is showing up without fear of condemnation. When we recognize that everyone has these different aspects of themselves, we can extend grace to others in their struggles while inviting them toward the healing that comes from living more consistently from their True Self.

The Four Selves: A Framework Born from Real Life

While Lewis B. Smedes' foundational work on the true self and false self in Shame and Grace provided valuable insight into identity formation, this Four Selves framework represents an expanded model that addresses a more comprehensive spectrum of how we show up in daily life. Where Smedes focused primarily on shame healing through the contrast of true and false selves, this framework provides a more comprehensive approach to understanding the various versions of ourselves that emerge in different circumstances, ultimately guiding us toward living more consistently from our True Self in Christ.

This framework didn't come from a textbook—it emerged from wrestling with how I responded differently to certain situations, and from observing the same response patterns in the lives of those I pastored. It was during my doctoral studies that I was able to give structure and language to what I had been observing, creating a practical framework that could help others understand their own identity patterns.

It's important to note that this Four Selves framework describes normal human adaptability and spiritual formation—not psychological pathology. We all naturally adapt our responses to different situations and relationships, which is healthy human behavior. This model provides a spiritual lens for understanding these natural adaptations within a Christian discipleship context, helping believers recognize when they're operating from security in Christ versus operating from wounds or performance pressure. This framework is not intended to diagnose, treat, or suggest any form of personality disorder or psychological condition.

Here's what I've learned:

Your Actual Self - The beautiful, messy reality of being human. This is you without filters, acknowledging both your brokenness and your belovedness, your struggles and your strengths. It's the version that says, "I'm struggling, and that's okay."

Your False Self - The wounded you, operating from fear and pain, using strategies that once helped you survive but now sabotage your ability to thrive. This is the version driven by lies about your worth and God's love.

Your Presentable Self - The curated you, carefully managing impressions and avoiding vulnerability to maintain an image you think others want to see. This version is exhausted from performing but terrified to stop. We often fear that if we're truly seen, we'll be rejected. Manning calls this the 'imposter'—the one we present to the world. But God doesn't love the mask. He loves the soul beneath it.

Your True Self - Who you were created to be before

wounds, performance, and fear distorted your reflection of God's image. This is you—secure in His love, naturally expressing His character through your unique personality and gifts. Your True Self emerges not when you're trying to be someone else, but when you're simply resting in whose you are.

Here's the liberating truth: your True Self is already complete in Christ. This isn't something you achieve through spiritual discipline—it's something you live FROM. This authentic you doesn't emerge through perfection, but through surrender. Every time you stop striving and start trusting, stop performing and start belonging, your True Self rises to the surface like a breath you've been holding finally released.

Dallas Willard reminds us that transformation is not about trying harder—but training wisely. The True Self is formed by abiding, not achieving.

Your True Self has been waiting patiently beneath every mask, every protective pattern, every false identity—not buried so deep you can't find it, but so close you've been looking past it. It's been there all along, whispering the truth about whose you are when the world's noise grows quiet enough to hear.

This is the you that God sees when He looks at you with delight. This is the you that naturally loves without keeping score, serves without exhaustion, and speaks truth wrapped in grace. This is who you are when you're home.

The goal isn't to eliminate the other selves—they're part of the human experience. The goal is to live more consistently from your True Self, the person God created you to be and is forming you to become.

How They Show Up in Your Daily Life

Once you start recognizing these patterns, you'll see them everywhere. Let me share some examples that might feel familiar:

At Work:

- **Actual Self:** "I made a mistake on that project. I need to own it and learn from it."
- **False Self:** "I can't let anyone see I'm struggling. I'll work late to fix this in secret."
- **Presentable Self:** "I'll craft an email that makes this look like someone else's fault."
- **True Self:** "I'll take responsibility gracefully and ask for help where I need it."

In Relationships:

- **Actual Self:** "I'm hurt by what you said, and I need to talk about it."
- **False Self:** "I'll shut down emotionally to protect myself from being hurt again."
- **Presentable Self:** "I'll pretend everything's fine and say what keeps the peace."
- **True Self:** "I can share my feelings honestly while still loving you well."

In Parenting:

- **Actual Self:** "I'm frustrated and need a moment before I respond."
- **False Self:** "I'll control this situation through anger or manipulation."

- **Presentable Self:** "I need to look like the perfect parent to other families."
- **True Self:** "I can set boundaries with love and teach through grace."

The beautiful thing about this framework is that it helps you understand yourself without condemnation. When you catch yourself operating from your False or Presentable Self, you don't have to shame yourself—you can simply redirect with grace.

A Biblical Picture: Peter's Journey Through the Four Selves

I love Peter's story because it shows us what this transformation actually looks like in real life. Peter wasn't perfect—he was gloriously, messily human, just like us.

Peter's Journey Through the Four Selves:

Peter's Actual Self - When he honestly admitted: "Depart from me! for I am a sinful man, O Lord" (Luke 5:8)

No pretense, just honest truth about his condition before God.

Peter's False Self - When he drew his sword in the garden, trying to fight his way out of God's plan.

Peter's Presentable Self - When he claimed he'd never deny Jesus, managing his image as the loyal disciple.

Peter's True Self - After Pentecost, when he boldly proclaimed Christ, secure in his calling despite his past failures.

The same Spirit who transformed Peter is working in you, helping your True Self emerge more consistently through every season of your life.

Just like Peter's journey shows us, this transformation isn't just a spiritual concept—it plays out in the most practical areas of our daily lives. Your body, soul, and spirit are constantly working together. Learning to recognize which self is leading, can change everything about how you experience each day.

How Your Body, Soul, and Spirit Work Together

Here's where it gets practical: learning to live from your True Self means recognizing when your body, soul, and spirit are working in harmony versus when they're in conflict.

When your True Self is leading:

- Your **body** relaxes into peace and authentic presence
- Your **soul** processes from truth rather than fear
- Your **spirit** communes freely with God

All three parts of you work together, creating a sense of alignment and authenticity.

Simple Steps for Daily Awareness

Rather than overwhelming you with complex techniques, let me share three simple practices that have transformed my daily experience:

Morning Intention: "Holy Spirit, help me live from my True Self today. Show me when other versions of me try to take control, and gently guide me back to who I really am in You."

Moment Pause: When you feel reactive, ask: "Which self wants to respond right now? What would my True Self—the person secure in God's love—do here?" Take three deep breaths before responding.

Evening Grace: "Where did I experience my True Self today? I celebrate Your grace working in me. Where did fear or performance take over? I receive Your forgiveness and ask for growth tomorrow. I surrender it all to You."

Remember, this isn't about perfection—it's about progression. Some days your True Self leads beautifully. Other days you catch yourself operating from wounds or masks and gently redirect. Growth happens in the catching, not in never struggling.

Summary: Your Four Selves Framework

Through this chapter, you've discovered that:

Who Am Eye? is expressed through which of the Four Selves leads your daily life. You are not defined by your struggling moments (Actual Self), your wounds (False Self), or your image management (Presentable Self)—you are defined by your True Self, the Christ-formed identity that emerges as you live from God's love and truth.

Whose Am Eye? remains constant regardless of which self shows up. You belong to the God who is patiently forming your True Self through every season, just like He did with Peter. Even when other versions emerge, you are still His beloved child, secure in His unchanging love and grace.

The Four Selves framework helps you recognize patterns without condemnation, understanding that Christ is transforming you progressively into who you really are.

Final Reflection

Before moving forward, let me ask you some honest questions:

1. **"Looking at your typical week, which of the Four Selves shows up most often—and in what situations?"**

2. **What specific triggers (criticism, conflict, pressure) tend to activate your False or Presentable Self?**
3. **Imagine living from your True Self for one whole day. How would your relationships, work, and inner peace be different?**

Call to Action

This week, practice these two essential steps:

Daily Self-Awareness: When you notice yourself reacting instead of responding, pause and ask: "Which self is leading right now?" Don't judge—just notice with grace.

True Self Anchoring: Each morning, remind yourself: "I am God's beloved child. Today I choose to live from this truth rather than from my wounds or need for approval."

Key Principle

Living from your True Self isn't about becoming someone new—it's about letting go of who you're not and embracing who Christ is forming in you through His perfect love.

Scripture Foundation

2 Corinthians 5:17 | Luke 5:8 | 2 Corinthians 10:9 | Ephesians 4:11-16 | Romans 10:4 | 1 Corinthians 13:11 | Philippians 1:6 | 2 Corinthians 5:17

Now that you understand the Four Selves framework, you might be wondering: 'I can see these different versions of myself showing up, but what do I do with all the emotions that surface when I start paying attention?'

In Chapter 6, we'll explore the crucial journey from numbing your emotions to courageously naming them—discovering that feeling is actually the pathway to freedom, not the obstacle to it.

As you continue this journey of discovering whose you are, remember that transformation happens not through self-effort but through surrender to the Holy Spirit's work within you. In Chapter 6, we'll explore what to do with the emotions that surface as you become more aware of your Four Selves.

Chapter 6

From Numbing to Naming - The Courage to Feel

"When thou passest through the waters, I will be with thee; and through the rivers, they shall not overflow thee: when thou walkest through the fire, thou shalt not be burned; neither shall the flame kindle upon thee." —(Isaiah 43:2)

From Relational Awareness to Emotional Courage

After discovering how your Four Selves operate in daily life in Chapter 5, you might be wondering: 'I can see these different versions of myself showing up, but what do I do with all the emotions that surface when I start paying attention to these patterns?

Here's what I've learned through my own journey: the pain you don't acknowledge will always shape your identity, usually in ways you don't want. When we understand that we belong to the God who entered our pain and became acquainted with grief, we can approach our emotions not with shame but with hope—and discover that feeling is actually the pathway to freedom, not the obstacle to it.

Numbing or Naming your pain

There's a moment in every healing journey where you have to choose between numbing your pain or naming it. For years, I chose numbing—and it directly affected which version of myself showed up in different situations.

When we numb our pain:

- Our **False Self** gets stronger (using distractions and defenses to avoid feeling)
- Our **Presentable Self** becomes more active (managing image to hide what's really happening)
- Our **Actual Self** gets buried (can't be honest about our real experience)
- Our **True Self** struggles to emerge (authentic connection requires emotional honesty)"

Too often we ignore our internal signals. As Willard Gaylin reminds us, our emotions are vital signs—meant to be listened to, not silenced. The False Self thrives by muting those signs.

I threw myself into work, achievements, even ministry activities—anything to avoid sitting still long enough to feel what was actually happening in my heart.

Maybe you recognize this too. Maybe you've become really good at staying busy, scrolling your phone, binge-watching shows, or filling every quiet moment with noise, because silence makes the hurt too loud. Maybe you've convinced yourself that spiritual maturity means being unaffected by pain, that "good Christians" should be able to pray their way past hurt, without actually dealing with it.

But here's the thing I wish someone had told me years ago: pain isn't failure—it's information. It's your soul trying to tell you something important about who you are and whose you are, like a warning light on your dashboard that you can't just ignore by putting tape over it.

Dan Allender calls pain "the narrow road" that God uses to shape our souls. When we avoid our hurt, we avoid the very places where God wants to speak healing.

We live in a culture—and often attend churches—that want to rush past pain, desperate for quick fixes and instant relief. We're taught that faith should make us bulletproof, that spiritual maturity means unshakeable emotions, that "real Christians" don't struggle with depression, anxiety, or deep hurt. But that's not biblical wholeness—that's emotional numbness, and it's not what God wants for your identity discovery.

Scripture shows us otherwise—Elijah experienced such deep depression he asked God to take his life (1 Kings 19:4), David cried out in anguish, "Why are you cast down, O my soul?" (Psalm 42:5), and even Jesus Himself was "troubled in spirit" (John 13:21) and experienced such distress that His sweat became like drops of blood (Luke 22:44).

Why We're Afraid to Feel

Most of us learned early in life that certain emotions weren't safe to express. Maybe your family communicated through criticism and sarcasm, shutting down authentic feeling. Maybe emotions were seen as weakness, teaching you to smile when you were dying inside. Maybe conflict meant someone was leaving, so you learned to avoid anything that felt too intense.

These patterns teach us to fear our own emotional experience and disconnect from what's happening in our hearts. But when we can't feel our pain, we also can't fully experience joy, intimacy, or God's comfort. Emotional numbing doesn't discriminate—when you shut down hurt, you often shut down everything else too.

Here's what we miss when we're afraid to feel:

We miss God's comfort. You can't be comforted for pain you won't acknowledge. When you numb your hurt, you rob yourself of experiencing God as your true Comforter.

We miss authentic connection. Relationships stay shallow when we can't share what's really happening in our hearts. People connect with our honesty, not our perfection.

We miss important information. Our emotions tell us when something's wrong, when we need help, when we're overwhelmed, when we need to set boundaries. Ignoring these signals is like driving with the dashboard warning lights covered.

We miss the full range of being human. God created us as emotional beings. When we try to live without feeling, we're rejecting part of how He designed us.

Jesus: Our Model for Entering Pain

Even Jesus—the Son of God, perfect and sinless—didn't avoid sorrow. He entered it fully. He wept over Jerusalem. He groaned in the garden. He cried out on the cross. "Jesus wept" —(John 11:35) is the shortest verse in the Bible, but it reveals something profound about how God views our emotional experience.

Notice how Jesus handled emotional pain:

- He felt it fully - When Lazarus died, Jesus didn't give a theological lecture; He wept

- He expressed it honestly - In the garden: "My soul is

exceeding sorrowful, even unto death" (Matthew 26:38)

- He brought it to the Father - His most intense emotions led to deeper prayer, not shutdown

- He trusted the process - Even in agony, Jesus trusted His Father's purpose

This is our model: Feel fully, express honestly, pray deeply, trust completely.

If Jesus didn't try to bypass pain, maybe discovering "Who Am Eye?" requires us to stop running from it too.

A Vision That Changed My Understanding of Surrender

Let me share how God showed me the connection between emotional avoidance and the False Self patterns we explored in Chapter 5. During my first year of doctoral studies, I had a vision that rocked my understanding of surrender.

I saw myself floating downstream in a river, but here's the thing—my body was completely immersed in the water, but I was keeping my head rigidly above the surface. I was white-knuckling control, terrified to let go completely.

The Lord showed me in that moment that I trusted Him with my salvation, but I was still relying way too much on my own understanding for everything else—including how I processed emotions. I was trying to manage my feeling process instead of surrendering to His.

This vision revealed a painful truth I'd been avoiding: my difficulty trusting anyone—including God—with my full emotional experience came from years of believing that feelings were dangerous, that vulnerability was weakness, that spiritual people should be above such "fleshly" experiences.

God was calling me to let go—to trust Him not just with my eternal destiny but with every broken, scared, angry, disappointed feeling that I'd been trying to manage on my own. It was an invitation to move from emotional self-protection to divine protection, from managing my pain to surrendering it.

And you know what happened when I finally allowed myself to feel the full weight of my disappointments, my fears, and all the ways I'd been trying to control my emotional experience? God met me in that vulnerability with His perfect love. The very thing I was afraid would destroy my sense of spiritual maturity, became the doorway to deeper intimacy with Him.

Learning to Feel Without Fear: The Psalms as Our Guide

The Psalms teach us how to process emotions from our True Self rather than our defensive patterns. David shows us that we can feel everything deeply while remaining anchored in whose we are. But here's the key: he brought all those feelings to God. He didn't pretend they weren't there, and he didn't let them have the final word about his identity.

Notice how David's emotional honesty actually strengthened his True Self:

He acknowledged raw feelings without shame (Actual Self honesty)

He refused to hide behind false spirituality (rejected Presentable Self pressure)

He brought his pain to God rather than numbing it (avoided False Self strategies)

He anchored his hope in God's character (True Self security)

David felt everything—rage at his enemies, despair when God felt distant, confusion when life didn't make sense, explosive joy when he experienced God's goodness. But here's the key: he brought all those feelings to God. He didn't pretend they weren't there, and he didn't let them have the final word about his identity.

Notice what David does here: he talks to his soul. He acknowledges the turmoil without shame, but then he redirects his hope toward God, and reminds himself whose he is. This is what healthy emotional processing looks like—feeling fully while anchoring your identity in truth.

Look at the emotional range in just a few Psalms:

Raw honesty: "I am weary with my groaning; Every night I make my bed to swim; I water my couch with my tears" (Psalm 6:6)

Fierce anger: "Break their teeth, O God, in their mouth: Break out the great teeth of the young lions, O Jehovah" (Psalm 58:6)

Deep depression: "My tears have been my food day and night, While they continually say unto me, Where is thy God?" (Psalm 42:3)

Overwhelming joy: "Thou hast turned for me my mourning into dancing; Thou hast loosed my sackcloth, and girded me with gladness" (Psalm 30:11)

David gives us permission to feel the full spectrum of human emotion, while maintaining our connection to God. He shows us that spiritual maturity isn't emotional flatness—it's emotional honesty combined with unshakeable trust in God's character.

When God Seems Silent in Our Pain

But what about those seasons when we're finally brave enough to feel our emotions honestly, but God seems silent in our pain? These quiet times often reveal which of our Four Selves we're trusting to handle the uncertainty.

Our False Self wants to control the silence, fill it with distractions, or force God to respond on our timeline. Our Presentable Self wants to pretend the silence doesn't affect us or that we're 'fine' with God's timing.

But our True Self can rest in the silence, trusting that God's love remains constant even when His voice feels distant.

Sometimes God allows the quiet, so that we can finally hear what our hearts have been trying to tell us all along. Our conscious mind gets skilled at burying our deepest fears and feelings, but in the stillness, truth has space to surface.

I've come to realize that His light shines brightest when I dare to visit the dark emotional places in my soul. God's heart as our Father is never to shame us in our emotional darkness, but to meet us there with His light and love. Like a tender father who enters his child's room during a nightmare, He comes not to condemn our fear but to comfort it, not to judge our sadness but to heal it.

St. John of the Cross spoke of the Dark Night of the Soul—those long, dry seasons when God feels emotionally distant. But in those nights, the soul learns to trust God's love beyond feelings, to know whose we are even when we can't feel His presence.

His silence isn't abandonment—it's His patient, loving presence giving us space to be honest about what's really going on in our hearts without the pressure to "feel better" right away.

The Difference Between Healthy Feeling and Unhealthy Wallowing

Learning to feel doesn't mean becoming controlled by emotions or getting stuck in painful feelings. There's an important distinction between healthy emotional processing and unhealthy emotional indulgence:

Healthy emotional processing from your True Self:

- Acknowledges emotions as information about what's happening in your soul
- Brings feelings to God for comfort and perspective
- Seeks to understand what the emotion is teaching you
- Maintains hope in God's goodness even while hurting
- Leads to growth, healing, and deeper intimacy with God

Unhealthy emotional wallowing from wounded patterns:

- Makes emotions the final authority about truth and identity
- Stays stuck in the feeling without seeking God's perspective
- Uses emotions to manipulate others or justify destructive behavior
- Loses hope and gets consumed by the pain
- Leads to isolation, bitterness, and spiritual decline

The goal isn't to eliminate pain—that's not possible this side of heaven. The goal is to process it in God's presence so it can teach us about His faithfulness rather than controlling our sense of identity.

When Churches and Families Teach Us to Avoid

Emotions

Many of us learned to fear our emotions in religious environments that prioritized appearance over authenticity. Maybe you heard messages like:

- "Christians should always have joy"
- "If you're struggling, you must not have enough faith"
- "Just pray about it and move on"
- "Your feelings don't matter—only God's truth matters"

These well-meaning but misguided messages create emotional shame and teach us that our internal experience is somehow unspiritual or unimportant to God. But this couldn't be further from biblical truth.

God created you as an emotional being. He gave you the capacity to feel deeply because that's part of bearing His image. When you honor your emotional experience by bringing it to Him, you're not being unspiritual—you're being human in the way He designed you to be.

The goal isn't to eliminate emotions from your spiritual life—it's to integrate them into your relationship with God so that your feelings become part of your worship, your honesty becomes part of your prayer, and your struggles become part of your testimony.

Practical Steps for Learning to Feel Without Fear

If you've spent years numbing or avoiding emotions, learning to feel can seem overwhelming. Here are some practical steps to begin this sacred work:

Start small. You don't have to dive into your deepest pain immediately. Begin by simply noticing what you're feeling throughout the day without trying to change or fix it. Ask: "Which of my Four Selves is reacting to this emotion?

Name it to tame it. When you feel something, practice putting a word to it: "I'm feeling anxious," "I'm feeling disappointed." Then ask: "Is this emotion coming from my True Self's honest assessment, or from old wounds and fears?

Ask God to meet you in it. Instead of asking God to take away the feeling, invite Him to be with you in it: "God, I'm feeling afraid right now. Will You be with me in this fear and show me what my True Self needs to remember?"

Remember: feelings aren't facts. Your emotions provide important information, but they don't determine ultimate truth about your identity or God's love for you.

Practice the pause. When strong emotions arise, resist the urge to immediately distract yourself or push them away. Take a few deep breaths and ask, "What is this feeling trying to tell me about which version of myself is taking over?"

Find safe people. Share your emotional experience with trusted friends who can listen without trying to fix or judge you.

The Sacred Work of Feeling

As we end this chapter, I want you to understand that learning to feel is sacred work. When you choose to acknowledge your emotional experience instead of numbing it, you're participating in God's design for human wholeness. You're choosing courage over comfort, authenticity over image management, connection over isolation.

This isn't about becoming an emotional mess or losing control of your feelings. It's about integrating your emotional life into your spiritual journey so that every part of you can experience God's love and healing.

You don't have to wait until you're "over it" to experience God's comfort. You don't have to pretend you're further along than you are to qualify for His grace. You are not failing in your spiritual journey by having feelings—you are being human in the way God created you to be.

The journey ahead won't always be comfortable, but it will be worth it. Because on the other side of acknowledged pain is authentic freedom. On the other side of named emotions is genuine healing. And on the other side of felt grief is deeper joy than you ever thought possible.

Final Reflection

1. **What emotions have you been numbing that might reveal which of your Four Selves has been protecting you from feeling?**

2. **How does knowing you belong to the God who entered our pain change how you approach difficult emotions?**

3. **When you're emotionally vulnerable, which self typically takes over—and what would it look like for your True Self to lead instead?**

Call to Action

This week, practice naming one emotion instead of numbing it. When feelings arise, bring them to Jesus in prayer rather than trying to manage them yourself.

Key Principle

The emotions you acknowledge in God's presence become the doorway to deeper intimacy with Him, and to living more consistently from your True Self. The feelings you avoid or numb, become barriers that keep you stuck in defensive patterns, rather than authentic identity.

Scripture Foundation

John 11:35 | Matthew 26:38 | Psalm 42:3 | Psalm 6:6 | Psalm 58:6 | Psalm 30:11 | Isaiah 43:2 | 1 Peter 5:7 | James 5:7 | Psalm 34:18 | Romans 8:28 | Hebrews 4:15-16 | 2 Corinthians 1:3-4 | Matthew 11:28 | Luke 4:18

Now that you understand how emotional courage connects to living from your True Self, you're ready to see how these patterns show up in your most important relationships. The emotions you've been avoiding often surface most powerfully when you're trying to love others well.

When we can't feel our own pain, we often can't truly connect with others' hearts either. But when we learn emotional courage in our relationship with God, it transforms how we love our family, friends, and community."

Chapter 7 will help you see how these patterns show up in your most important relationships. We'll discover how emotional honesty becomes the foundation for authentic connection and how your True Self transforms the way you love others.

Chapter 7

How Your Four Selves Show Up in Relationships

From Self-Awareness to Relationship Healing

After discovering how your Four Selves operate in daily life in Chapter 5, you might be wondering: "How does this actually play out when I'm trying to love my spouse well, navigate conflict with my teenager, or figure out why certain people trigger me so intensely?"

Here's what I've learned after years of watching relationships—including my own—succeed and fail: our relationships become mirrors that reflect not only what we value, but also which version of ourselves is leading when we love, argue, or attempt to connect. More importantly, they reveal whether we're living from the security of knowing whose we are or from the insecurity of not knowing our true worth.

When we understand that we belong to the God of perfect love—the One who models authentic relationship within the Trinity itself—we can approach our human relationships with both hope and honesty.

A Personal Confession: My Relational Journey

I approach this chapter not from a place of relational perfection, but from the humility of someone who has experienced both the beauty and brokenness of human relationships. My own journey has included seasons of deep connection and painful loss, which has taught me that our relationships become mirrors reflecting not only what we value, but which version of ourselves is leading when we love, argue, or attempt to connect."

But God's mirror is completely different. When painful relationships have taught us that we're unlovable, disappointing, or 'too much,' we start believing those distorted reflections are true. We see ourselves through the lens of rejection, criticism, or abandonment.

God's mirror shows us something entirely different. When He looks at you, He doesn't see your relational failures or the wounds others have inflicted. He sees who you're becoming through His grace—His beloved child, being transformed day by day into the image of Christ.

Where Your Different Selves Show Up in Love

Using the Four Selves framework from Chapter 5, think about your closest relationships for a moment. Can you identify which version of yourself tends to show up?

When Your Actual Self is leading in

Relationships: You're honest about both your strengths and struggles without using them to manipulate. You might say: "I'm feeling hurt by what happened earlier, and I need to talk about it. I also want to understand your perspective." You seek authentic connection rather than perfect chemistry, and you're willing to work through conflict instead of avoiding it or steamrolling through it.

When Your False Self is leading in Relationships: You find yourself performing, controlling, or withdrawing based on old wounds and fears. You might become the people-pleaser who says yes to everything to avoid rejection, or the controller who attempts to micromanage everyone's emotions to feel safe. You're constantly monitoring the emotional temperature of the room, scared that if people see the real you, they'll leave.

When Your Presentable Self takes over: You become an expert at managing impressions and avoiding anything that feels too vulnerable or risky. You say what you think people want to hear rather than what's actually true for you. Conversations stay safely on the surface because depth feels dangerous. You might present a "perfect family" image while hiding real struggles.

But When You Begin to Live from Your True Self: Something beautiful happens: relationships become places of grace rather than arenas of performance. You can show up as yourself—flawed, growing, honest—and trust that real love can handle reality. You can set boundaries without guilt, love without keeping score, and be present without trying to control outcomes.

The Impossible Burden We Place on Others

Here's something that opened my eyes about relationships: I had to learn that no human being can heal the wounds that shaped my False and Presentable Selves. When we expect another person to complete us or fix our childhood hurts, we set them up to fail—not because they don't love us, but because they were never meant to be our Savior.

This is such a common pattern, and it connects directly to the Four Selves framework. Your Actual Self carries those unmet childhood needs. Your False Self develops elaborate strategies to get those needs met through performance or control. Your Presentable Self carefully curates an image designed to attract the kind of love you've always craved.

Psychologist Carl Jung captured this perfectly: "The unconscious purpose of choosing a marital partner is to complete childhood."

But here's the truth that set me free: this expectation is completely unrealistic and utterly unfair. When we expect another human being to heal our childhood wounds or meet our deepest needs, we set them up to fail—not because they don't love us, but because they were never meant to be our Savior.

I had to learn this the hard way. For years, I believed that if I could just be needed by others, I wouldn't be rejected. This belief shaped how I showed up in every relationship—I gave more than I had to give, thinking it would earn love and loyalty. But being needed is not the same as being known. And being useful is not the same as being loved.

The True Self, secure in God's love, can enter relationships with open hands rather than grasping fists. You can love without needing something back, serve without keeping score, and be present without trying to control outcomes.

The Wounds That Shape How We Love

Let me share how understanding the Four Selves framework

helped me break a generational pattern that was affecting my relationships with my children. A childhood abandonment wound at age 13, had created relational patterns I was unconsciously passing down, until God showed me how to interrupt the cycle.

This wound at times drove me to perform for approval, avoid conflict to prevent abandonment, use achievement to establish my worth in relationships, and display anger to keep people at a distance when vulnerability felt too risky. I was relating from my wounds—desperately trying to earn through performance what I believed love required, rather than simply receiving the unconditional acceptance that love actually offers.

Understanding this completely shifted how I show up in relationships. I no longer need to impress to connect. I don't have to be the smartest person in the room or the most successful or the most spiritual. I can simply be present, and that's enough. (We'll explore the specific details of how wounds create identity patterns in Chapter 8.)

Breaking the Patterns We Inherited

Something that might surprise you: many of the unhealthy patterns we carry in relationships aren't even originally ours. They're passed down through generations like heirlooms we never asked for.

Maybe your family communicated through criticism and sarcasm. Maybe love was conditional on achievement. Maybe conflict meant someone was leaving, so you learned to avoid it at all costs. Maybe emotions weren't safe to express, so you learned to smile when you were dying inside.

These patterns shape how we see ourselves and others until God intervenes with healing. The wounds we inherit don't have to define our future—God wants to heal not just you, but your family tree. The unhealthy patterns that have been passed down for generations can stop with you when you let Him love you whole.

Beverly Tauke reminds us that some of our internal struggles are echoes of inherited pain. Healing begins when we trace the roots and allow God to rewrite the legacy.

My Mountain Experience: Breaking Generational Patterns

One of the most vulnerable things I've ever done as a father required me to face my own wounds head-on, so I could stop passing them down to my sons.

As a young father, the impact of growing up without a dad wasn't immediately obvious. Without a model for fatherhood, strictness became the default whenever uncertainty arose in parenting situations. Rules and regulations felt safer than exploring the unknown boundaries of what a father should and shouldn't allow. The truth is, I didn't know how to be a father myself.

What my children needed more of, was a father who could calm their storms, just like Jesus did for His disciples. The disciples learned to trust in the calm steadfastness of Jesus—He was their anchor. I realized, what my children needed, was the same calming presence when storms were raging in their little lives.

The Lord gently revealed to me that I couldn't give my kids what I had never received. Trust had to be passed down, but it had to start with me learning to trust my Heavenly Father.

One day, I took my boys up a mountain—not to speak, but to listen their souls back into life. The terrifying step was asking them to share everything they felt I had failed them in, as as a father. I promised them no retaliation, no justification, and no defensiveness. They needed to feel safe enough to speak their truth and know they would be heard.

That mountain became more than a location—it became a sacred moment of breaking a generational pattern of emotional cutoffs in my family. I had to name my own father wound and its impact on my parenting, before I could offer my sons something different.

The revelation came that parenting couldn't be done for the Holy Spirit—it had to be done with Him. And that shift, only came when I stopped trying to parent from my wounds and started parenting from the healing God had given me.

Without the Holy Spirit, I wouldn't have been able to give my sons the security I had never known how to receive. He was the One restoring what I had never learned how to offer.

My Personal Journey: Learning to Love from Wholeness

When Relationships Became Performance

For years, I found myself exhausted by relational patterns I couldn't understand. I would:

- Over-give to earn approval (False Self trying to prevent abandonment)
- Avoid difficult conversations to keep peace (Presentable Self managing image)
- Take responsibility for others' emotions (False Self trying to control outcomes)
- Feel drained after social interactions (performing instead of simply being present)

As I learned to live from my True Self—secure in God's

love rather than seeking it through relationships—everything changed. I could finally serve from fullness rather than emptiness, love without keeping score, and be present without trying to fix everyone around me.

The Healing That Changed Everything

Through prayer, honest conversations with mentors, and a lot of uncomfortable self-awareness, I began experiencing what it meant to be loved without condition. I learned that I didn't have to be perfect to be precious, didn't have to perform to be accepted.

As I learned to trust God's fatherly love—really receiving it in my heart, not just knowing it in my head—I could offer that same love to others. I no longer needed to fix everyone around me or constantly prove my worth by being needed. I could finally serve from fullness rather than emptiness.

The Ripple Effect

This transformation made me a safer father, friend, and pastor. When you know whose you are, one can love others without losing yourself. You can be present without trying to control outcomes. One can care deeply without carrying burdens that aren't yours to bear.

What Your Relationships Are Telling You

Take a moment to consider: What are your current relationships revealing about the condition of your soul?

Maybe you notice you're exhausted from trying to manage everyone's emotions. That might be fear trying to control outcomes to feel safe.

Maybe you realize you haven't had a truly vulnerable

conversation in months because you're too busy maintaining your image. That could be shame keeping you isolated while appearing connected.

Or maybe you're starting to recognize moments when you love without needing anything back, when you speak truth with kindness, when you're fully present instead of protecting yourself. Those are glimpses of the person Christ is forming in you breaking through.

Here's what I want you to remember: We don't need perfect relationships—we need honest ones. God's grace meets us in our relational brokenness and teaches us to love from wholeness, rather than woundedness.

Practical Steps for Loving from Your True Self

Before Important Conversations: Pause and ask yourself, "Which self is about to show up right now?" Notice your patterns without judgment, and invite your True Self—the version of you that's secure in God's love—to lead the way.

When You Feel Triggered:

- **Recognize:** "My False Self wants to control this situation"
- **Pause:** "Let me take a breath before responding"
- **Connect:** "Holy Spirit, help me respond from love, not fear"
- **Choose:** "What would my True Self do here?"

Daily Relationship Practices:

- Listen to understand, not to respond
- Speak truth wrapped in grace

- Love without needing something back
- Serve from overflow, not obligation

Moving Forward Together

The relationships in your life are sacred mirrors that reveal which version of yourself is leading. When you learn to love from your True Self—secure in God's love rather than seeking it through others—you create space for authentic connection and healing.

But here's what I've discovered: our relational patterns often trace back to specific wounds that created our defensive strategies. Understanding these wounds is crucial for breaking free from cycles that keep us stuck.

Final Reflection

Before we move forward, consider these questions:

1. **Which of the Four Selves shows up most frequently in your closest relationships?**
2. **What childhood wounds or family patterns are you still carrying into your adult relationships?**
3. **How has God's love been healing your capacity to love others well?**
4. **Choose one specific relationship: What would it look like to love that person from your True Self this week?**

Call to Action

This week, practice the "which self" pause, before three significant conversations. Identify one inherited family pattern you want to break. Choose one relationship where you'll practice loving from security rather than need. Share one authentic struggle with a safe person instead of managing your image.

Key Principle

Relationships become sacred mirrors when we see them through God's eyes. The goal is authentic love—loving from our True Self rather than our wounds, performance, need for approval, or need to be right.

True love doesn't control—it releases. It doesn't shame—it nurtures. It doesn't demand perfection—it offers grace.

Scripture Foundation

Matthew 5:44 | Hebrews 10:25 | 1 Corinthians 4:26 | Proverbs 20:19 | John 15:45 | Matthew 22:37-39 | Romans 12:15 | Ecclesiastes 4:9-12 | Colossians 3:14 | 1 Peter 4:8 | Ephesians 4:2-3 | 1 John 4:19

In Chapter 8, we're going to take a holy pause. Now that you've seen how your Four Selves show up in relationships, you're ready to look deeper at the specific wounds that created these patterns. Before diving into the healing work ahead, we'll look honestly at where you are right now—through God's eyes—and prepare your heart for the transformation that's waiting for you.

Chapter 8

THE WOUNDS THAT SHAPE OUR FOUR SELVES

"The deepest wounds we receive in life are often the very places where God wants to bring His greatest healing and use us to heal others."

Dan Allender

From Relationship Awareness to Wound Identification

After seeing how your Four Selves show up in relationships, the natural question becomes: 'Where did these patterns come from? What created the defensive strategies I rely on?'

This is where we move from recognizing patterns to understanding their origins. When we can name our specific wounds, we begin to understand which version of ourselves developed as protection—and why certain situations trigger us so intensely.

Understanding the connection between your wounds and the Four Selves framework from Chapter 5, is like having a map for your healing journey. Instead of being confused by why you sometimes feel like a stranger to yourself, you can begin to trace those patterns back to their source and invite God's healing into those specific places.

Here's what I've discovered through my own painful journey: the False Self doesn't form in a vacuum—it forms in response to specific wounds that taught us lies about who we are. Your Presentable Self develops elaborate strategies to avoid the kind of vulnerability that led to past pain. Your False Self builds protective walls around the tender places where you were hurt. Meanwhile, your True Self—the person God created you to be—remains buried beneath these survival mechanisms.

Let me be clear: ambition, drive, and success aren't bad things. God gives us gifts, talents, and opportunities to excel. The question isn't whether you achieve—it's why you achieve.

Are you building, creating, and succeeding from the security of knowing whose you are? Or are you driven by a desperate need to prove your worth?

Healthy Achievement (True Self motivated):

- Flows from calling and stewardship of God-given gifts
- Success enhances life but doesn't define worth
- Motivated by serving others and glorifying God
- Can handle setbacks without identity crisis
- Success enhances life but doesn't define personal worth

Wound-driven Achievement (False Self motivated):

- Desperately needed to answer "Who am I?
- Success becomes the foundation of identity
- Motivated by fear, insecurity, or proving value
- Failure feels like a direct threat to worth

When success flows from knowing whose you are, it becomes stewardship and service. When it's driven by wounds, it becomes a prison—no matter how golden the bars appear.

To truly walk in the freedom of knowing whose we are, we must return to those wounds with Jesus—not to relive the pain, but to finally tell the truth about what happened and how it's been determining which version of ourselves emerge in different situations. When we understand which wounds drive which versions of ourselves, we can stop being controlled by unconscious reactions and start making conscious choices about who we want to be.

For some, this may feel scary. Believe me, I've been there. But when you understand whose you are—a beloved child of the Father who sees every wound and desires to heal them all—you find the courage to name what hurt you. We belong to the God who chose to be wounded on the cross for our healing, who takes our deepest pain and transforms it into His greatest tool for ministry and redemption in others' lives.

Why Naming Specific Wounds Matters for Identity

Here's the truth that changed everything for me, and as Dr. Rob Reimer says: "We cannot heal from what we refuse to name." To heal, we must name what we've tried to hide. As Kaufman teaches, when shame is brought into relationship—into care—it loses its power. But more than that—we cannot discover who we really are while operating from unnamed wounds.

Your wounds don't just hurt you once and fade away. They keep speaking, whispering lies that you often mistake for truth about your identity. Until we name them and invite God's truth into those specific places, they continue shaping which version of ourselves shows up.

Here's how specific wounds create specific false identity patterns and determine which self shows up:

Abandonment wounds often create a False Self that desperately tries to control outcomes, to prevent being left again. This version of you might become clingy, performance-driven, or hypervigilant about relationship security. Your Presentable Self might become the "low-maintenance" person who never asks for anything to avoid being seen as too much trouble.

Rejection wounds frequently develop a Presentable Self that carefully manages impressions to avoid criticism. You become skilled at reading rooms, saying what people want to hear, and hiding parts of yourself that might not be accepted. Your False Self might become the people-pleaser who says yes to everything, or the achiever who tries to earn love through performance.

Shame wounds typically create a False Self that hides behind anger, defensiveness, or isolation to protect against exposure. Your Presentable Self becomes an expert at deflection, keeping conversations surface-level, and maintaining an image that covers the parts of yourself you believe are unacceptable.

Betrayal wounds often produce a False Self that trusts no one and assumes the worst about people's motives. Your

Presentable Self might become the strong, independent person who never admits need or vulnerability, while secretly longing for connection but being terrified to risk it.

A child who never hears "You matter" may grow into an adult whose False Self performs for worth, constantly asking "Who am I?" through achievements, while their Presentable Self carefully curates an image of success to hide their deep fear of being insignificant.

A teenager whose trust is shattered may become someone who keeps everyone at arm's length—including God—because they've forgotten whose they are.

A person who experiences abandonment might spend their whole life trying to prove they're worthy of staying, never resting in the security of belonging to the God who never leaves.

But here's the thing: these wounds don't just hurt us once and then go away. They keep speaking, whispering lies that we often mistake for truth about our identity. And Satan doesn't hold back from reminding us of these lies, using our wounds against us whenever we're most vulnerable in our sense of worth.

The wound whispers things like: "You're not enough, and you never will be" "You always mess things up—that's just who you are" "You don't really matter to anyone" "You'll always end up alone"

If we don't recognize those whispers for what they are—lies born from wounds that contradict God's truth about our identity—we start building our entire sense of self around them. But Jesus came to expose those lies with His truth about who we are and whose we are.

How My Father Wound Created My False and Presentable Selves

As I shared in Chapter 7, a childhood abandonment wound became the toxic driver behind my adult identity patterns. Let me go deeper into how this specific wound shaped the different versions of myself that would emerge.

I was 13 years old when I went to live with my mother, and my father told her he wouldn't pay child support. I can still remember the thought that went through my mind: "I must not be very significant to him. I must not be worth much."

That wound—that deep sense of not being chosen, not being worth fighting for—didn't just hurt once and fade away. It created specific default behavioral patterns that would show up in different situations, each one trying to protect me from ever feeling that worthless again:

My False Self spent decades trying to prove that I was worth something through wealth and success. This version whispered, "If you can just achieve enough, accumulate enough, accomplish enough, no one will ever be able to abandon you again because you'll be too valuable to lose."

My Presentable Self became the successful businessman who always had it together, who never showed need or vulnerability, who carefully managed his image so that people would see someone worth keeping around. This version was terrified that if people saw my real struggles or needs, they might decide I wasn't worth the investment.

My True Self—the beloved son who was chosen by God before the foundation of the world—remained buried beneath these other versions for decades, surfaced only in moments of worship or prayer when I felt safe enough to be authentic.

By September 2004, I was a multimillionaire after selling two of my businesses. I was king of my own little kingdom, and I thought I'd finally answered the "Who am I?" question with success. But God had a very different story in mind for revealing my true identity.

What I've learned: when we don't deal with our wounds,

we end up building our entire identity around trying to prevent them from happening again. I thought wealth and success would make me invulnerable to abandonment and finally answer who I was. But the deeper work of healing was still ahead of me.

How Wounds Create Distorted Lenses About Identity

Unnamed wounds don't just hurt—they change how we see ourselves and God. Think of it like wearing glasses with the wrong prescription. Everything looks blurry, distorted, out of focus.

Your wounds become the lens through which you interpret:

- How God sees you
- Whether you're worth loving
- What you need to do to be safe
- How much you can trust others

Here's how specific wounds create specific identity distortions:

Rejection wounds make us interpret love as obligation. Instead of receiving love as a gift that affirms our worth, we assume people only care about us because they have to or because we're useful to them.

Abandonment wounds make us fear closeness. We want intimacy, but we keep people at a distance because getting close means risking being left again, which would confirm our worst fears about who we are.

Shame wounds make us sabotage grace. When God offers us His unconditional love, we find ways to disqualify ourselves because grace feels too good to be true for someone like us.

Betrayal wounds make us suspicious of trust. We become hypervigilant, always watching for signs that people will let us down, which becomes a self-fulfilling prophecy that confirms our fears.

Performance wounds make us believe love is conditional. We exhaust ourselves trying to earn what was always meant to be freely given, never resting in the security of unconditional acceptance.

I couldn't renew my mind about my identity while I was still seeing life through the broken lens of that 13-year-old boy, who felt worthless. God had to help me identify that lens, name where it came from, and choose to see my identity through His truth instead.

Identifying Your Core Wounds

Now comes the practical work of identifying the specific wounds that shaped your defensive patterns. Ask yourself these questions with God's help:

What recurring emotional reactions do you have?

- Do you panic when people seem upset with you? (Possible rejection wound)
- Do you feel worthless when you make mistakes? (Possible shame wound)
- Do you become controlling when things feel uncertain? (Possible abandonment wound)
- Do you shut down when conflict arises? (Possible trauma wound)

What lies do you hear in difficult moments?

- "You always mess things up"
- "No one really wants you around"
- "You can't trust anyone"
- "You're not worth fighting for"
- "If people really knew you, they'd leave"

Which of your Four Selves shows up most often?

- If your **False Self** dominates: What is it protecting you from?
- If your **Presentable Self** is always "on": What are you afraid people will see?
- When does your **Actual Self** feel safe to emerge?
- How often do you experience your **True Self** leading?

What patterns did you inherit?

- How did your family handle emotions, conflict, or vulnerability?
- What unspoken rules governed your household?
- What did you learn about earning love and

acceptance?

The Connection Between Wounds and Your Four Selves

Understanding how specific wounds create specific patterns helps us make sense of why different versions of ourselves show up in different situations. When you can trace your reactive patterns back to their source, you stop being confused by your own behavior and start having compassion for the wounded parts of yourself that are just trying to protect you.

Here's what I want you to understand: your wounds aren't your fault. But healing them is your responsibility. And the beautiful truth is that you don't have to do this work alone. God wants to meet you in every painful place and show you how loved you truly are.

The goal of naming your wounds isn't to assign blame or wallow in past pain. It's to understand how those experiences shaped the lies you've been believing about your identity so you can invite God's truth into those specific places. When we understand which wounds drive which versions of ourselves, we can stop being controlled by unconscious reactions and start making conscious choices about who we want to be.

Bringing Your Specific Wounds to the Father

Here's where the real identity transformation happens. Once you've named your wounds, bring them to your Heavenly Father. He's not afraid of your pain, surprised by what hurt you, or disappointed that you still struggle with the effects of old wounds on your sense of worth.

Here's how to bring your specific wounds to Him for

healing: Be honest about the pain, confess the lies you believed about your identity, and ask for His truth to replace those lies. This isn't a one-time prayer—it's an ongoing conversation as God heals you layer by layer.

Breaking Generational Patterns: Taking My Sons Up the Mountain

One of the most powerful aspects of wound healing is realizing that the unhealthy patterns that have been passed down for generations can stop with you when you let God love you whole.

Many of the wounds we carry aren't even originally ours. They're inherited patterns of pain, passed down through family lines like toxic heirlooms we never asked for. But God wants to heal not just you, but your family tree.

When you choose to heal from your wounds rather than pass them down, you become a generational pattern breaker. The lies that shaped your parents don't have to shape your children. The defensive strategies that your family relied on don't have to become your legacy.

As I shared in Chapter 7 about my mountain experience with my sons, one of the most personal examples of how I learned to name wounds and break generational identity patterns happened the day I took my boys up a mountain—not to speak, but to listen their souls back into life and show them their true worth.

The deeper work behind that mountain experience was recognizing how my own father wound had created patterns I was unconsciously passing down. I had to do the hard work of naming how my abandonment wound had shaped my False Self (the strict, rule-focused father) and my Presentable Self (the pastor who couldn't show weakness or need). Only then could I offer my sons something different—the security of knowing their worth wasn't performance-based.

Without the Holy Spirit, I wouldn't have been able to give my sons the security I had never known how to receive. He was the One restoring what I had never learned how to offer—the unshakeable knowledge of being beloved sons.

As we move forward in this journey, remember that every wound you name in God's presence becomes a doorway to deeper intimacy with Him. The places where you've been most broken often become the places where you can most powerfully help others discover their true worth. Your healing journey isn't just for you—it's for everyone God will bring into your life who needs to know that transformation is possible.

Hope for Transformation: You Are Not Alone

What you're doing right now is incredibly brave and meaningful. You're walking the same path every person who has experienced deep healing has traveled. Remember: God is not overwhelmed by your wounds, you don't have to do this perfectly, and transformation happens in His presence, not through your performance.

Through this chapter, you've discovered that:

Who Am Eye? is often distorted by unnamed wounds that create false patterns and defensive strategies. When you can identify the specific wounds that shaped your False and Presentable Selves, you begin to understand why certain situations trigger you and which version of yourself takes over in different circumstances.

Whose Am Eye? becomes clearer as you bring your wounds to the God who specializes in healing broken hearts. You belong to the One who was wounded for your healing, who takes your deepest pain and transforms it into His greatest tool for ministry in others' lives.

Your wounds are not your identity—they're experiences that God wants to heal and use for His glory and others' good.

Final Reflection

1. **What specific wound has most shaped how you see yourself?**
2. **Which of your Four Selves developed in response to that wound?**
3. **How is God inviting you to bring this wound to Him for healing?**

Call to Action

This week, ask God to show you one specific wound that still affects your identity. Name it honestly and invite Him into that painful place for healing.

Key Principle

When you understand which wounds shape your False and Presentable Selves, you can begin living more consistently from your True Self—the beloved child who knows exactly whose they are.

Scripture Foundation

John 6:37 | Romans 8:38 | Psalm 147:3 | Isaiah 43:4 | Luke 4:18 | 2 Corinthians 1:3-4 | Romans 8:37 | Psalm 147:3 | Isaiah 61:1 |

Genesis 50:20 | Genesis 45:22-24 | Numbers 6:24-26 | Matthew 11:28 | Hebrews 4:15-16

Now that you've courageously named the wounds that shaped your defensive patterns, you're standing at a crucial crossroads. Awareness is powerful, but it's only the beginning. In Chapter 9, we'll explore what it means to stand at the sacred threshold between knowing what needs to heal and choosing to step forward into that healing.

Chapter 9

Standing on the Step - The Sacred Threshold of Change

"We are not necessarily doubting that God will do the best for us; we are wondering how painful the best will turn out to be."

C.S. Lewis

From Wound Identification to Taking the Step

After courageously naming the wounds that shaped your defensive patterns in Chapter 8, you now find yourself at a pivotal moment. You know what hurt you, you understand how it created your False and Presentable Self strategies, and you've invited God into those painful places.

But now comes the crucial question: Will you choose to step forward into the healing God has for you, or will you stay where it feels familiar and safe?

You're standing on what I call the sacred threshold—the

decision point between awareness and transformation, between knowing what needs to change and actually changing it. This isn't just another milestone in your journey; this is the moment that will determine whether your pain becomes your prison or your pathway to freedom.

Every person I've walked alongside in ministry eventually arrives at this same crossroads. Some people take the next step and experience breakthrough. Others stay where they are and wonder why their lives never really change. The difference isn't ability, intelligence, or even faith—it's the willingness to move when God says move.

When we know whose we are, we discover that God meets us wherever we are, not to condemn us for being there, but to give us courage for what's next.

The Long Journey

Before we dive into the sacred work of stepping forward, I want you to understand something profound: every moment in this journey is sacred. You've been doing the hard work of learning to listen to your heart, growing in your ability to acknowledge your pain, and courageously naming the wounds that shaped your protective patterns. You've been looking honestly at the lies you've believed and continuing the process of surrendering them to God's truth.

This isn't work you complete once and move on from—it's an ongoing journey of discovery. Some days you'll feel clear about your identity; other days the old patterns will resurface and you'll need to remember whose you are all over again. Some seasons you'll walk confidently in your True Self; other times you'll catch yourself slipping back into old protective modes and gently redirect your heart toward truth.

But here's the beautiful hope I want you to hold onto: as

you learn to rest in Jesus and surrender these false patterns, it genuinely becomes easier over time. You'll find yourself catching your self-talk more quickly, recognizing which of the Four Selves is trying to take the lead before you react. The redirection back into God's grace becomes more natural as you learn to trust the Holy Spirit's gentle guidance.

What once felt like an exhausting battle gradually transforms into a graceful dance of surrender, where you're partnering with God rather than striving in your own strength.

That's not failure—that's the normal rhythm of transformation. You're not trying to arrive at some perfect place where you never struggle with identity questions again. You're learning to live from the security of knowing whose you are, even when the journey of discovering who you are continues to unfold.

That's not small work—that's holy work. And now you're standing at the threshold between who you've been and who God is calling you to become.

Dr. Martin Saunders often reminded us that transformation requires what he called "holy pauses"—moments when we stop the frantic pace of trying to fix ourselves and simply stand still long enough to hear God's voice about what comes next. This isn't delay—it's preparation. This isn't procrastination—it's positioning yourself to move when the Spirit says move.

Think about Jesus in the garden before His crucifixion. He didn't rush toward the cross. He paused. He prayed. He wrestled with His Father about what was coming. And in that holy pause, He found the strength to say: "Nevertheless not my will, but thine, be done" (Luke 22:42).

That pause didn't delay His mission—it prepared Him for it.

You're in your own garden moment right now. The healing work ahead will require courage you don't feel like you have, trust you're not sure you can muster, and surrendering control in ways that terrify you. But this holy pause—this sacred threshold—is where God meets you with everything you need for what's next.

When Everything I Built Came Crashing Down

Let me share with you the moment when I found myself at this exact threshold—when all my awareness about my father wound and my patterns of proving my worth suddenly collided with a crisis that would change everything.

As I mentioned in Chapter 8, my father wound had driven me to build wealth and success as proof of my worth. But God had a very different story in mind.

In 2004, I owned a supermarket, and what I initially thought was someone illegally washing cars in my parking lot turned out to be something far more serious. The man wasn't just washing cars—he was a drug lord using the operation as a front for his dealers to plant drugs in vehicles.

Over time, I discovered he had been behind a series of armed robberies at my supermarket on several occasions over a six-month period. What I had dismissed as a minor nuisance became a life-threatening confrontation. When this drug lord threatened my life, something broke inside me—not just my sense of control, but my entire identity.

Standing in my own store that morning, I realized that all the wealth I'd accumulated to protect myself from abandonment, all the success I'd built to prove my worth, all the control I'd maintained to feel secure—none of it could save me from this moment. Everything I thought defined me was powerless.

That's when I faced my sacred threshold. I could keep trying to fight, to control, to protect what I'd built. Or I could finally surrender everything to the God I'd been trying to serve while still being king of my own kingdom.

I fell to my knees and cried out, "Lord, I'm done fighting You. I surrender my entire estate to You."

In that moment, everything changed. Not because my circumstances immediately improved—they got much worse before they got better. But because I finally chose to trust God with my identity instead of protecting it myself.

The bank repossessed my home and truck. I remember walking to the store while friends drove past in their Mercedes, some giving me the cold shoulder. I was no longer the successful businessman they admired. I was no longer the guy who had it all figured out. I was no longer anyone I recognized.

That day, walking down that street with nothing left, I cried out, "Lord, who am I?" I was no longer the rich man. I was no longer the achiever. I was no longer the person who could protect himself through wealth and power. All my answers to "Who am I?" had been stripped away.

But here's what I discovered in that stripping away: when everything I thought defined me was gone, what remained was who I really was—God's beloved son, chosen not for what I could achieve but for whose I was.

The next day, I enrolled at Hebron Theological Seminary and began studying theology. Over the following three months, I mourned the loss of my business, my image, and the death of the arrogant man I had become. But in that mourning, I began the real journey of discovering who I truly was in Christ—not a successful businessman protecting himself from abandonment, but a beloved son of the King whose worth was never in question.

This experience showed me how God can use even traumatic circumstances to strip away our False Self and reveal our True Self. But more than losing my external securities, I had to surrender my warped lens—a lens that had been shaped by years of circumstances, wounds, and failures. Through this distorted lens, I could only see myself as a failure, a man who had lost everything that mattered.

What I didn't see at the time was that God's lens was perfect, and He could see my True Self beyond all my failures. He was looking at His beloved son and calling me chosen.

This is what it meant to discover "Who am Eye?" through surrender. The question shifted from "Who am I?" to "Whose am I?" And that made all the difference.

When we lose everything we thought defined us, we don't lose ourselves—we find ourselves. We discover that our identity was never dependent on our circumstances, our achievements, or our ability to control outcomes. Our identity is anchored in the unchanging love of the God who calls us His own.

Why Change Feels So Hard

Let me share with you why transformation can feel like an uphill battle: C.S. Lewis captures exactly what people feel when standing at the threshold of change—we're not necessarily doubting that God will do the best for us; we're wondering how painful the best will turn out to be.

Our minds naturally gravitate toward the path of least resistance. When we try to grow spiritually, we should expect inner resistance—and sometimes even pushback from people around us who've grown comfortable with the old version of us.

When you start living differently, it challenges other people's comfort zones and forces them to confront their own need for transformation. This resistance is normal and expected. People have a vested interest in keeping you in the box they've created for you. When you step out of that box, it can be unsettling for those around you.

That's why lasting transformation requires intentionality. If we're not purposeful about our spiritual growth, any change we experience won't stick. It's like trying to change the course of a river—without consistent effort, the water will find its way back to the familiar path.

What gives me tremendous hope is witnessing people make significant life changes through small, consistent steps. Just 1% growth at a time. And 1% plus 1% plus 1%—added up over months and years—leads to what I call remarkable transformation. This is sustainable change, the kind that lasts because it's built on a foundation of gradual, Spirit-led growth rather than willpower alone.

What makes spiritual growth different from simple behavior modification is that we're not just trying to change our actions—we're partnering with God for authentic heart transformation.

The Hidden Cost of Standing Still

But let me share something most people don't want to talk about: staying where you are isn't neutral—it's a choice with consequences. I've watched people remain stuck in the same patterns for years, even decades. Their pain doesn't stay the same—it compounds. That unforgiveness you're carrying doesn't just affect you; it seeps into how you parent your children, how you treat your spouse, how you show up at work.

When you refuse to take the next step God is calling you to, you don't just miss out on growth—you miss out on the fullness of life He wants to give you. Without realizing it, you become a teacher of your wounds, instead of your healing, passing down the same patterns, the same fears, the same limitations to the people you love most.

I know this sounds harsh, but it's the truth I wish someone had told me years earlier: every day you choose familiar pain over unfamiliar freedom is a day you rob yourself and others of the breakthrough God has waiting.

But here's the beautiful truth that balances this hard reality: God's grace meets you exactly where you are, and His love doesn't diminish, based on how long you've been stuck, or how many times you've chosen comfort over growth. He's patient with your process while also calling you forward into freedom.

How to Partner With God in Your Healing

Now that you've named your wounds and understood their connection to your Four Selves, it's time to learn how to actively partner with God in your transformation. This isn't about willpower or trying harder—it's about surrendering to the healing process He wants to lead you through.

Step 1: Ask God to reveal what He wants to heal. Pray and ask, "Holy Spirit, which wound are You ready to heal in me today?" Don't force it—let Him bring specific memories or patterns to mind. He knows what you're ready to handle and when.

Step 2: Name the wound without justifying or minimizing it. Simply acknowledge what happened: "When I was [age], [specific event] happened, and it hurt me." This isn't about blame—it's about truth. And truth, even painful truth, is what sets us free.

Step 3: Identify the lie it planted about your identity. What did that experience teach you about your worth? About whether you can trust people? About whether God really cares? Name the specific lie that took root.

Step 4: Acknowledge how it's still affecting your

identity. How does that wound show up in your current sense of self? Your view of God? Your relationships? Which version of yourself tends to take over when this wound gets triggered?

Step 5: Listen for God's voice, not pain's voice. Here's something crucial: pain doesn't just hurt—it speaks about our identity. And the problem is, we often confuse the voice of pain with the voice of truth. This is where the question "Whose am I?" becomes essential—when we remember we belong to God, we can distinguish His voice from every other voice trying to define us.

Pain's Voice: "You're broken and always will be." **God's Voice:** "You're beloved and being made whole."

Pain's Voice: "You'll never change—this is just who you are." **God's Voice:** "I'm not finished with you yet."

Pain's Voice: "You deserved what happened to you." **God's Voice:** "You are precious in My sight."

We have to learn to test every voice against the truth of Scripture about our identity. The voice that speaks with love, hope, and redemption is the voice of the One we belong to.

Step 6: Bring it directly to your Heavenly Father. Here's where the real transformation begins. Be completely honest about the pain: "Father, when this happened, it made me feel worthless/afraid/angry/abandoned." Confess the lies you believed: "Because of this wound, I've believed that I'm not worthy of love." Ask for His truth to replace the lies: "Show me how You see me. Replace these lies with Your love."

Step 7: Choose forgiveness and release. "I choose to forgive [person] for what they did. I also forgive myself for the ways in which I've responded from this wound." This isn't a feeling—it's a choice to release the right to revenge, and trust God with justice. Forgiveness is an act of obedience and surrender to who God knows us to be. When we forgive, we're not excusing the wrong or pretending it didn't hurt—we're choosing to live from our True Self, the version of us that belongs to the God of mercy and grace.

Remember: Jesus won't take from you what you don't give to Him. He's not a bully who forces healing on us. We're invited to cast our burdens on Him, not cradle them forever. But when we do surrender them, He doesn't just take our pain—He transforms it into something beautiful.

The Heart vs. Mind in Sustainable Change

Here's something I've discovered through my own struggles and years of ministry: we can change our minds many times about the same issue, but we cannot change our hearts. That's God's territory, and we need His intervention for true heart transformation—especially when it comes to forgiveness.

You can change your behavior through willpower and determination, but sustainable transformation requires a change of heart through God's grace. Your mind can decide to forgive someone, but only God can remove the sting of bitterness from your heart. Your mind can resolve to love differently, but only the Spirit can produce the kind of love that flows naturally and consistently.

This is why Jesus said: "I am the vine, ye are the branches: He that abideth in me, and I in him, the same beareth much fruit: for apart from me ye can do nothing" (John 15:5).

Real transformation, the kind that lasts, requires divine partnership. You bring your willingness; God brings His power. You offer your open hands; He changes your heart.

A Biblical Picture: Peter's Journey

I love Peter's story because it shows us what gradual, Spirit-led transformation actually looks like. From his bold declaration "Thou art the Christ, the Son of the living God" Matthew 16:16

to his devastating denial "I know not the man" Matthew 26:74, Peter's path was marked by both spiritual victories and painful failures.

But Jesus never gave up on Peter's transformation. After the resurrection, Jesus asked Peter three times: "Lovest thou me?" (John 21:15) not to shame him, but to restore him incrementally, one declaration at a time. Each "yes" became a step toward the man God was forming.

The same Peter who cowered before a servant girl later stood boldly before thousands, declaring: "Let all the house of Israel therefore know assuredly, that God hath made him both Lord and Christ, this Jesus whom ye crucified" (Acts 2:36).

This wasn't overnight transformation—it was the fruit of surrendered, Spirit-led growth over time.

Here's what encourages me about Peter's story: his failures didn't disqualify him from his calling. Instead, they became part of his preparation for it. The same can be true for you.

The Step I Had to Take: When Two Words Changed Everything

Let me share with you the most difficult and transformative step I ever had to take in my healing journey. It taught me that forgiveness isn't just a matter of faith—it's a commandment from our Master.

Jesus made this clear when He said: "So ye also, when ye shall have done all the things that are commanded you, say, We are unprofitable servants: we have done that which it was our duty to do" (Luke 17:10).

There's a reward in forgiveness, and God's smart—He knows what's best for us, even when we can't see it.

One quiet morning during my prayer time, the Holy Spirit spoke something to my heart that I never saw coming: "Forgive your father."

We had been estranged for twenty-three years. Twenty-three years! And now, Lord, You want me to forgive him? I was so shaken that I immediately called my mentor Trevor Walker. "What do I do?" I asked, hoping he'd give me an easy way out.

He paused—one of those long, thoughtful pauses that mentors do when they're about to change your life—and said just two words: "What if?"

I waited, expecting him to finish his sentence. But then it dawned on me what he was doing. Trevor's two words weren't giving me an answer—they were creating space for me to stand on that sacred threshold and truly consider what forgiveness meant. He gave me room to step into my own decision rather than telling me what to do.

And suddenly, the "what ifs" started flooding my mind:

What if my children ask me about forgiveness someday and I never forgave my own father? What if I stand in the pulpit preaching about forgiveness while harboring unforgiveness in my own heart? What if I miss God's plan because I'm holding onto this pain?

Those two words haunted me all day.

The next morning, I did something that terrified me—I tracked my dad's address and arranged to meet with him that weekend. When I saw him, everything about the encounter felt surreal. Here I was, 6 foot 1, and he seemed so much smaller than I remembered. This man who had loomed so large in my childhood trauma now looked fragile, almost vulnerable.

For a split second, a dark thought crossed my mind: "I would love for you to try what you did when I was a child, now that I'm bigger than you." But I pushed that aside and told him why I was there: "Dad, I came to forgive you."

The look on his face was unforgettable—like a deer staring into headlights. Then he did something that made my blood boil: he pretended not to know what I was talking about. The rage that filled my mind was so intense, I knew I had to leave before I did something I'd regret forever.

As I drove away, I was furious—at him, at the situation, even at God. "Lord," I said, "I did what You asked me to do, and I'm done with him."

But God wasn't done with me.

A couple of months later, my father reached out asking if I had a couch he could use. Can you believe that? Twenty-three years of no contact, I offer forgiveness, he denies everything, and then he asks for furniture. I was still processing that when, three years later, my sister called with news that would change everything.

"Dad is dying," she said quietly.

My immediate response was cold: "Your dad is dying. Mine died a second time three years ago."

But my sister, with the grace only a sister can have, said, "Well, I wanted to give you the opportunity to decide for yourself what to do."

Once again, I found myself calling Trevor. And once again, guess what he said? "What if?"

That man and his two-word wisdom.

So there I was, walking into a third-world hospital to see the man who had abandoned me, now lying on his deathbed. I hardly recognized him with an oxygen mask covering his face. His eyes were closed, and I stood there watching him—the man who had shaped so much of my pain without even being present.

Then our eyes met.

In those few seconds, his eyes spoke volumes—more remorse than a thousand words could ever express. A single tear rolled down his cheek, and something shifted in my heart. I needed to see that tear. I needed to know that somewhere, somehow, he understood the pain he had caused.

I stayed that entire day, doing things for my father that he had never done for me as a child. The hospital was understaffed, so I helped with his basic needs—feeding him, adjusting his position, making sure he was comfortable. And the whole time, I'm talking to God: "Lord, now You even have me doing things for him, that he didn't do for me when I needed a father. I'm angry at You and I'm angry at him."

But I heard those gentle words in my spirit: "Just do it."

So I did.

The next day I was scheduled to take a tour group to Israel—something I'd been planning for months. Before I left, I knew this would be our final conversation on this side of eternity. I leaned close to him and asked, "Dad, have you got your affairs worked out with the Lord?"

He slowly nodded his head.

"Dad, I'm glad to hear that, because I didn't get to know you much on this side of life, but I look forward to getting to know you in heaven." Then I said the words that I knew God wanted me to say: "I want you to know that I forgive you, and I release you to die in peace."

Another tear rolled down his eye.

As I drove away from that hospital, I was honest with God about where my heart still was: "Lord, I said that I forgive him, but I need to feel it in my heart. My mind has forgiven him, but my heart isn't there yet."

What happened in that hospital room was my True Self leading the way. The forgiveness I offered my father came from the deepest, most authentic part of who I am in Christ. It felt good to offer him that forgiveness. Not because he deserved it, but because it flowed from who God created me to be. My True Self knew this was right, even when my emotions were still catching up.

But then, sitting in my truck afterward, my Actual Self took over—the honest, unfiltered part of me that acknowledged the gap between what my spirit had done and what my heart was still processing. That's when I poured out my real feelings to God, admitting I needed His help to align my emotions with my obedience.

Three days later, I was leading my tour group through Israel when my mom sent me a text that stopped me in my tracks: "Your dad has passed."

We were on a bus heading to En Gedi when something unexpected happened. I suddenly started weeping—not just crying, but the kind of deep, uncontrollable weeping that comes from somewhere you can't access on your own. I buried my head between my legs, trying not to make it obvious to my tour group members.

After several minutes of this overwhelming grief, I whispered to God through my tears: "Lord, why am I weeping like this? I don't understand what's happening to me."

And then came that gentle whisper that changed everything I understood about forgiveness: "Because you asked Me to help you feel it in your heart."

That moment on a bus in Israel, was the very first time I cognitively became aware that God could do something in my heart that I was completely unable to do for myself. He had taken my obedience and transformed it into heartfelt forgiveness.

Here's the beautiful mystery of how the True Self works—when you step out in authenticity and surrender, God uses that moment to prepare your soul for healing that may come years later. My True Self's act of forgiveness in that hospital, opened the door for my soul to receive this revelation about God's heart transformation, years later on that bus.

The obedience came first; the full understanding and heart healing followed in God's perfect timing.

This Taught Me Something Profound About "Who Am Eye?"

I discovered that when I live from my True Self, even when my emotions haven't caught up yet, God honors authenticity and uses it to transform hearts.

Forgiveness is a process, and our obedience to forgive releases us from chains that bind us to our pain, while revealing who we really are—children of the God who forgives.

When Others Won't Recognize Your True Identity

Here's something you need to be prepared for: not everyone will celebrate your transformation. Sometimes family members, friends, or colleagues will resist your growth and unconsciously try to pull you back into old patterns. They've grown comfortable with the old version of you, and may feel threatened by the changes they see.

This resistance is normal and expected. People have a vested interest in keeping you in the box they've created for you. When you step out of that box, it challenges their own identity and forces them to confront their own need for transformation.

Remember these truths when facing resistance:

- You don't need everyone's approval to live in your true identity
- Some people may never see or acknowledge the change—that's their limitation, not yours
- Stay consistent in living from truth regardless of others' responses

- Give people time to adjust to the new you; transformation can be unsettling for those around you
- Find community with others who celebrate your growth and support your journey

Most importantly, keep choosing to live from God's truth about who you are, regardless of whether others see it or celebrate it.

The One Thing You Can't Avoid Forever

More often that not, there's a decision that God keeps bringing you back to—the one you've been avoiding. It might be the conversation you need to have, the forgiveness you need to offer, the truth you need to face about yourself, or the dream you need to pursue.

You know what yours is. You've felt the Holy Spirit's gentle nude. You've probably made excuses, found distractions, or convinced yourself that you're "not ready yet." But that decision isn't going away—it's the doorway to everything God wants to do in and through your life.

The enemy wants you to believe it's too big, too scary, too complicated. But I've discovered that the decision itself is never as hard as the fear of making it. Most of our resistance isn't about the choice—it's about what we imagine might happen if we choose.

This is where Trevor's two-word wisdom becomes life-changing again. What if you make that choice and fail? Then you'll learn something valuable, and make the next choice wiser. What if it's harder than you thought? Then you'll discover God's strength in your weakness.

But Trevor taught me to flip the question: The real question isn't "What if I make this choice?" It's "What if I don't?"

Your Defining Moment

As we conclude this chapter, understand this: you are standing at a defining moment that will shape not just your future, but the future of everyone you love. Each choice you make brings you closer to your true identity—who Christ is forming in you.

Right now, ask yourself: What is the specific decision God has been asking you to make? What is the one thing you've been avoiding, postponing, or making excuses about?

Maybe it's forgiving someone who deeply hurt you. Maybe it's having an honest conversation about something you've been hiding. Maybe it's stepping into a calling that terrifies you. Maybe it's getting help for something you've been managing alone.

The decision God is calling you to make isn't just about your healing—it's about the healing you'll be able to offer others. The freedom you gain will become the freedom you can help others find. The chains you break will be the same chains you can help others break.

Standing at this crossroads means:

Acknowledging where you are without shame. You're not here by accident. God can use exactly where you are as a launching pad for where He wants to take you.

Accepting that everything brought you here for a divine purpose. Your wounds, your mistakes, your struggles—none of it has been wasted. God is weaving it all into your story of redemption.

Believing that this moment can become your breakthrough. What feels like a stuck place can become the very foundation for transformation.

Choosing to trust Him with the outcome. Faith isn't knowing where you're going; it's trusting the One who's leading you there.

This is the essence of knowing "Whose Am I." We belong to the God who works all things together for our good, even when we can't see how.

The choice you make today will become the story you tell tomorrow. Every testimony of transformation started with someone who was scared but chose anyway. You don't have to see the whole staircase—you just have to take the next step. God will meet you there with exactly what you need.

Where you are right now is not your destination—it's your decision point. Choose grace. Choose growth. Choose the God who never gives up on your transformation. Choose to live from the truth of whose you are, and watch as who you are, begins to align with His heart for you.

What will you choose today?

Final Reflection

Declaring Your New Beginning

1. **What specific step is God asking you to take that you've been avoiding?**

2. **How has understanding your wounds helped to see which self has been leading in difficult situations?**

3. **What would it look like to trust God with one decision you've been trying to control?**

Call to Action

This week, identify the one decision God has been asking you to make that you've been avoiding. Take one specific step toward that decision, trusting God with the outcome.

Key Principle

The sacred threshold between awareness and transformation requires both divine grace and human choice. God provides the power, but we must provide the willingness to step forward in faith.

Scripture Foundation

Philippians 1:6 | Romans 8:28 | Isaiah 43:19 | John 15:5 | Matthew 16:16 | Matthew 26:74 | John 21:15 | Acts 2:36 | 2 Corinthians 5:17 | Luke 17:10 | Luke 22:42 | Genesis 50:20 | Genesis 45:22-24 | Numbers 6:24-26

When you recognize the sacredness of the step you're on, you give yourself permission to grow. You no longer stay stuck in cycles of shame and self-rejection—you move forward in grace.

But taking that step requires more than courage—it requires breaking free from the specific lies that have been blocking your path. In Chapter 10, we'll explore how to identify and break agreement with the deceptions that keep you stuck, and how to embrace the truth that sets you free.

Chapter 10

Breaking Free from the Lies We've Believed

"Self-rejection is the greatest enemy of the spiritual life because it contradicts the sacred voice that calls us the 'Beloved.' Being the Beloved expresses the core truth of our existence."

Henri J.M. Nouwen

Trading Lies for Truth

After courageously standing at that sacred threshold in Chapter 9 and feeling the weight of choosing your next step, you're probably wondering: "Okay, I'm ready to move forward. But what exactly am I moving toward? What does taking that step actually look like in my daily life?"

Here's what I've discovered through my own journey and years of walking alongside others: the step forward almost always involves a divine exchange—trading the lies your wounds taught you, for the truth that Christ declares over your life. This isn't just about changing your thinking; it's about discovering who you really are beneath the deception, and remembering whose voice you're meant to listen to.

This is where "Who Am Eye?" and "Whose Am Eye?" become intensely practical. Every lie you believe creates a false answer to "Who am I?"—making you think you're worthless, broken, or disqualified. But every lie you break, reveals more of who you actually are in God's eyes. And when you learn to recognize whose voice is speaking (God's truth vs. the enemy's lies), you discover the security of knowing whose you are.

The problem is, the lies we believe about ourselves have become so familiar they feel like truth. They've been our constant companions for so long—whispering through painful experiences, echoing through hurtful words, reinforced by our own inner critic—that we've built our entire identity around them. But when we know whose we are—beloved children of the God of truth—we can courageously face these lies and exchange them, for His declarations over our lives.

This exchange is the difference between staying stuck where you are and stepping into the freedom that's been waiting for you.

How Lies Take Root

Lies rarely announce themselves with fanfare. They don't kick down the door shouting, "Here I am to destroy your life!" Instead, they slip in quietly during our most vulnerable moments—when we're hurt, scared, or ashamed—and they whisper things that almost make sense given what we're experiencing.

A child who feels responsible for their parents' divorce can grow into an adult who believes they ruin everything they touch. A teenager who gets rejected by their first love can become someone who sabotages relationships before they can feel abandoned again. A young person who's told they're "not smart enough" can carry that limitation into every opportunity for the rest of their life.

These lies take root when pain is never properly processed, and truth is never invited into the wounded places. Over time, they become what Scripture calls strongholds—deeply entrenched ways of thinking, that resist God's truth about who we are.

"For the weapons of our warfare are not of the flesh, but mighty before God to the casting down of strongholds; casting down imaginations, and every high thing that is exalted against the knowledge of God, and bringing every thought into captivity to the obedience of Christ" (2 Corinthians 10:4-5).

But here's what gives me hope: if lies can build strongholds, truth can tear them down.

How Lies Feel True

The most destructive lies feel true because they don't arrive with obvious deception. The most dangerous lies are the ones that feel true because they're based on real experiences that genuinely hurt us. These lies don't contradict our feelings; they seem to explain them.

When a father abandons his family, the lie whispers, "You must not be worth staying for." When a spouse betrays their marriage vows, the lie insists, "You'll never be enough for anyone." When a trusted leader fails, the lie declares, "You can't trust anyone, not even God."

These lies feel logical given our circumstances. They provide a twisted form of comfort because they give us someone to blame (usually ourselves) and create an illusion of control. If we can just be better, perform more, achieve enough, maybe we can prevent future pain.

But here's the truth that will set you free: these lies aren't insights about who you are—they're false interpretations that distort your identity. They're not revelations about reality—they're reactions to pain that haven't been surrendered to God's healing truth.

Here's where the question "Whose Am Eye?" becomes crucial. When you're in pain, whose voice are you listening to? The voice that says you're defined by what happened to you, or the voice of the One who says you're defined by His love for you? Every lie whispers a false answer to "Who am I?" but God's truth reveals who you really are beneath the pain.

I learned something life-changing early in my ministry: whatever you agree with shapes you. When you agree with shame, you wear it like a heavy coat. When you agree with fear, you live under its shadow. But when you agree with God's truth about you, you're transformed by it.

The prophet Amos asked a profound question: "Shall two walk together, except they have agreed?" (Amos 3:3).

You can't walk with God into the freedom He has for you while agreeing with lies about yourself. Something has to give, and it's usually our agreement with those lies that needs to be broken. When you stop agreeing with lies about who you are, you start discovering who you actually are. When you choose to listen to God's voice instead of deception's whisper, you remember whose you are.

The Power of What You Agree With

Think about it: What lies have you been agreeing with about who you are? Maybe it's "I'll never be enough" or "If people really knew me, they'd walk away" or "God must be disappointed in me." These aren't just random thoughts; they're false answers to "Who am I?" that you've accepted as truth, and they're shaping how you see yourself and how you relate to God and others.

But here's where God's truth will set you free. These lies didn't come from the God who created you and calls you His own. They came from wounds, from shame, from the enemy who wants to steal your identity. When you learn to recognize whose voice is speaking, you can choose which voice to agree with.

Fighting Lies with Truth

Here's the liberating reality: you have authority over what you agree with. You don't have to accept every thought that enters your mind as truth. You can test every voice against God's Word and choose which agreements you'll embrace.

"Casting down reasonings, and every high thing that is exalted against the knowledge of God, and bringing every thought into captivity to the obedience of Christ" (2 Corinthians 10:5).

This is spiritual warfare, but it's not fought with swords and shields; it's fought with truth. Every lie that contradicts what God says about you is an enemy stronghold that must be taken captive and replaced with His truth.

While James Clear writes from a secular standpoint, his principles reinforce my theological emphasis on sanctification as a daily process of being conformed to the image of Christ. His identity-based habit model aligns with Romans 12:2 and 2 Corinthians 3:18—being transformed by the renewing of the mind.

Here's how this works practically:

When the lie whispers: "You're too broken to be used by God" **You take it captive by saying:** "The Lord is nigh unto them that are of a broken heart, and saveth such as are of a contrite spirit" (Psalm 34:18).

When the lie says: "You'll never change" **You counter with:** "Being confident of this very thing, that he who began a good work in you will perfect it until the day of Jesus Christ" (Philippians 1:6).

When shame declares: "God is disappointed in you" **You respond with:** "There is therefore now no condemnation to them that are in Christ Jesus" (Romans 8:1).

This isn't just positive thinking; this is spiritual warfare using the sword of the Spirit, which is the Word of God.

The Four-Step Exchange

Here's a practical process I've used in my own life and taught to countless others for breaking agreement with lies and establishing agreement with truth:

Step 1: Name the lie specifically and identify whose voice it represents. Don't be vague. What exactly have you been believing about who you are? For example: "I have believed that I am worthless" or "I have believed that I always mess things up." Then ask: "Whose voice taught me this? This isn't how my Heavenly Father sees me."

Step 2: Renounce it in Jesus' name. "In Jesus' name, I renounce this lie and break my agreement with it. I refuse to let this deception define who I am any longer. This is not my identity—this is not whose I am."

Step 3: Speak the biblical truth about your identity. Find Scripture that directly reveals who God says you are and declare it: "God says that I am fearfully and wonderfully made, chosen before the foundation of the world, and deeply loved.

This is who I am because this is whose I am."

Step 4: Declare your new agreement with God's voice. "I choose to believe what God says about who I am rather than what my wounds or shame whisper. I agree with heaven's truth about my identity. I belong to the God of truth, and His voice defines me."

Let me give you an example of how this might sound in prayer:

"Lord Jesus, I have believed the lie that I am a failure and that nothing I do ever works out. I recognize this isn't Your voice speaking over my identity—this is the voice of shame and past wounds. In Your name, I renounce this lie and break agreement with it. Your Word says I can do all things through Christ who strengtheneth me, that all things work together for good to them that love God. This is who I am because this is whose I am—I belong to the God who calls me more than a conqueror. I choose to believe what You say about my identity rather than what my fear whispers. Holy Spirit, help me walk in this truth daily. Amen."

When Lies Fight Back: Remember to Work With the Lord

I need to warn you about something: when you start challenging lies with truth, they often seem to fight back. The enemy doesn't give up strongholds easily, and your mind is comfortable with familiar thought patterns, even destructive ones.

Don't be surprised if the lies seem louder for a while after you start this process. That's normal. It's like cleaning out a wound; sometimes it hurts more before it heals.

But here's the truth: if you keep feeding the bad wolf of lies, it will reign in your life. But if you feed the truth through God's

Word and His presence, peace will reign instead.

Here's how to stay strong when lies fight back:

Persist in speaking truth: Don't let resistance stop you from declaring God's Word over your life.

Increase your time in Scripture: Fill your mind with so much truth that lies have no room to take root.

Get community support: Let trusted friends speak truth over you when you can't hear it yourself.

Pray for the Holy Spirit's work: Ask Him to write truth in your heart and mind: "Holy Spirit, please write Your truth deep in my heart and mind. Help me not just to know it intellectually, but to believe it with everything in me. Make Your truth more real to me than the lies I've believed."

Be patient with the process: The lies took time to establish their hold; truth may also take time to fully establish its reign.

Truth Isn't Just Information—It's Encounter

Here's something that transformed how I approach this whole process: Truth isn't just a concept; Truth is a Person. Jesus said, "I am the way, and the truth, and the life: no one cometh unto the Father, but by me" (John 14:6).

When you receive truth, you're not just changing your beliefs; you're encountering Jesus Himself. His truth doesn't just inform you; it transforms you through relationship with Him. This is why you can read all the right books, memorize all the right verses, and still feel stuck; because transformation happens through encounter, not just information.

I remember the exact moment when God's truth about my worth moved from my head to my heart. I was in prayer, overwhelmed by a mistake I had made, when I felt His presence wash over me with this whisper: "You are My beloved son, in whom I am well pleased; not because of what you do, but because of who you are."

That wasn't just a nice thought; that was an encounter with the Truth Himself. And everything changed from that moment forward.

This is how "Who Am Eye?" gets answered through relationship, not just information. I discovered who I really was not through studying about God's love but through experiencing it. My identity shifted from "the pastor who has to be perfect" to "the beloved son who is perfectly loved." When you encounter Jesus as Truth, you don't just learn facts about yourself—you discover whose voice you were created to listen to and who you really are when that voice defines you.

This is why spending time with Jesus is so crucial to breaking free from lies. As you grow in your relationship with Him, His truth about you becomes more real than the lies you once believed. You stop trying to convince yourself of what you know intellectually and start experiencing what's actually true about you.

Why Today Matters: The Urgency of This Exchange

I feel a need to caution you, friend: every day you delay this exchange of lies for truth is a day you remain smaller than God created you to be. The lies aren't going to magically disappear on their own. They're not going to get bored and leave. They're going to keep whispering, keep limiting you, keep robbing you of the life God has for you until you actively choose to break agreement with them.

The step you identified in Chapter 9—the one God has been asking you to take—is probably being blocked by a lie right now. Maybe your step is:

- Starting that difficult conversation, but the lie says

"You'll just make things worse"

- Pursuing that calling, but the lie whispers "You're not qualified"
- Setting that boundary, but the lie insists "People will reject you"
- Forgiving that person, but the lie argues "They don't deserve it"

The longer you wait to face these lies, the stronger they become. But here's the beautiful truth: the moment you break agreement with a lie and choose God's truth instead, that lie loses its power over you forever.

Your Moment of Truth

The step you identified in Chapter 9 is probably being blocked by a lie about who you are right now. But here's what I want you to understand: you don't have to wait until you feel ready. You can take that step right now, armed with God's truth about who you are and secure in whose you are.

Your identity is not determined by what happened to you, what you've believed about yourself, or which voice has been loudest in your head. Your identity is determined by what the God of truth declares over you—and He calls you His beloved, His chosen, His own.

The freedom you've been longing for is on the other side of this divine exchange. When you trade lies for truth, you don't just get better thoughts—you discover who you really are. Choose truth. Your True Self is waiting.

Summary: Breaking Free from Deception

Through this chapter, you've discovered that:

Who Am Eye? becomes clear as you break agreement with the lies that have been creating false answers to this question. When you renounce deception and choose God's truth instead, you discover who you really are beneath the lies—His beloved child, chosen and secure.

Whose Am Eye? is settled when you learn to recognize God's voice above every other voice trying to define you. You belong to the God of truth, whose declarations over your life are more real than any lie you've believed.

The lies you break today become the freedom you walk in tomorrow.

Final Reflection

As we conclude this exploration of breaking free from lies, I want you to contemplate these questions. Don't rush through them. Let God speak to your heart as you consider each one:

1. **What lie has been whispering to you most persistently about your identity or worth?**

2. **How has this lie shaped your relationships with others and with God?**

3. **What would change in your life if you truly believed God's truth about you instead of the lies you've carried?**

Call to Action

This week, use the four-step process from this chapter to break agreement with one specific lie and choose God's truth instead:

Identify and Renounce: Name one specific lie you've been believing about yourself and break agreement with it in Jesus' name.

Replace with Truth: Find Scripture that directly contradicts the lie, memorize it, and ask the Holy Spirit to make His truth more real than the deception.

Key Principle

The lies you believe become the prison walls that limit your life. But when you break agreement with deception and choose God's truth instead, those same walls crumble and become stepping stones to the freedom Christ gave you on the cross.

"If therefore the Son shall make you free, ye shall be free indeed" (John 8:36).

Scripture Foundation

"And ye shall know the truth, and the truth shall make you free"(John 8:32).

John 14:6 | 2 Corinthians 10:4-5 | Amos 3:3 | John 8:32 | John 8:36 | Psalm 34:18 | Philippians 1:6 | Romans 8:1 | Romans 8:28-39 | Psalm 139:14 | Philippians 4:13 | 2 Corinthians 10:5 | 2 Corinthians 12:9 | 1 John 4:4

You've acknowledged the pain, named its source, stood at the step of change, and now you're breaking free from the lies that have held you back. But before we move into the final phase of reclaiming your identity, Chapter 11 invites you to take a sacred pause—to step back and see your transformation journey through God's loving eyes, celebrating how far you've come and preparing your heart for what's ahead.

Chapter 11

A Sacred Pause - Reflecting on Your Journey Through God's Eyes

"Spiritual formation is the process by which the inner reality of the person takes on the character of Jesus."
Dallas Willard

From Breakthrough to Sacred Reflection

After learning to break agreements with lies and choosing God's truth in Chapter 10, I want you to take a deep breath with me. You've been doing some of the most life-transforming work a human soul can do—facing pain, naming wounds, making exchanges that require tremendous courage, and actively breaking free from deceptions that have shaped your identity.

Now comes a crucial moment that will determine whether your transformation becomes temporary insight or lasting spiritual formation: the sacred pause to see your journey through God's loving eyes. This isn't delay—this is the discipline that deepens transformation and establishes patterns of continued growth.

When we know whose we are—beloved children of the eternal God—we need quiet reflection time to understand "Who Am Eye?" and "Whose Am Eye?" by seeing through His perspective above our problems.

Putting on God's Perfect Prescription Lenses

Before we move into boldly declaring who you are, I want you to imagine putting on a pair of prescription lenses—not just any lenses, but God's perfect prescription. When you've worn the wrong prescription for years, everything appears blurry, distorted, out of focus. But the moment you put on the correct lenses, suddenly everything snaps into crystal-clear focus.

For too long, you've been looking at your identity through the wrong prescription—lenses clouded by shame, scratched by wounds, distorted by lies. But God wants to give you His perfect prescription, to see what HE sees about your transformation journey.

The prescription in God's lenses corrects:

- **Shame-distorted vision → See beloved child**
- **Fear-blurred sight → See secure identity**
- **Performance-clouded view → See accepted son/daughter**

Through God's perfect lens, you can see three essential perspectives that will revolutionize how you understand your identity journey.

David's Model: Upward Focus, Inward Reflection Under God's Grace

Let me show you the first lens through King David's example. Picture him as a young shepherd boy, lying on his back in the fields, night after night, looking up at an endless canopy of stars. While his sheep grazed peacefully, David would gaze upward and meditate on the God who created every star he could see.

Listen to how he captures this: "When I consider thy heavens, the work of thy fingers, the moon and the stars, which thou hast ordained; What is man, that thou art mindful of him? and the son of man, that thou visitest him?" (Psalm 8:3-4).

David was wrestling with his own version of "Who Am Eye?" as he looked at God's vast creation. In the face of infinite stars and endless skies, David asked the ultimate identity question: "What is man?" But his question wasn't born from insecurity—it was born from wonder that the God who created all this magnificence would care about one small shepherd boy.

But David didn't just admire God's creation—he looked honestly at his own heart. When he made devastating mistakes, he cried out with brutal honesty: "Create in me a clean heart, O God; and renew a right spirit within me" (Psalm 51:10).

David's honesty about his failures never made him forget whose he was. Even in his darkest moments of moral failure, David could cry out to God with confidence because he knew he belonged to a Father who specializes in heart transformation. He understood that his identity wasn't based on his perfection but on God's faithfulness.

David's Model teaches us: Focus upward on God's greatness while looking honestly inward at your heart. The same mighty Creator who created all those stars called David "a man after His own heart" (1 Samuel 13:14), because he was willing to cry out honestly to a holy God, but also a loving Father.

The Lake Reflection: Seeing Past Surface Distortions to Your True Identity

Here's the second lens: learning to see past life's surface ripples to the true you that lies beneath.

I'll never forget standing at a lake's edge, watching my reflection change with every ripple. The image moved, blurred, and shifted with each small wave. My clothing looked different, my face seemed to change shape, even my posture appeared altered. But I knew that beneath all those surface distortions, I was still the same person.

This is a perfect picture of the identity confusion we all experience. When circumstances throw stones into the waters of our existence—grief, trauma, loss, failure—the ripples grow larger, dramatically changing how we perceive ourselves. Suddenly we don't recognize the person looking back at us. We start asking "Who am I?" based on the distorted reflection instead of the reality underneath.

But here's the truth: those ripples are not the real you. They're temporary distortions on the surface of who you actually are.

Your failures, your wounds, your mistakes, your struggles—these are experiences you've had, not your identity. They may have created ripples on the surface, but they haven't changed who you are underneath.

God sees past all the surface disturbances to the real you—the True Self He's been forming through Christ. While you're looking at the ripples and feeling confused about your identity, He's looking through them, to the person He created you to be, and is restoring you to become.

The Lake Reflection teaches us: the circumstances that have caused distortions—trauma, rejection, failures, wounds—are not your identity. They're experiences you've had, not who you are. When you learn to see through God's eyes, you discover that your True Self has been there all along, unchanged by the storms on the surface.

The Balcony Perspective: God's View From Above Your Problems Reveals Your Purpose

Here's the third lens: understanding that God looks down from above on all your problems with perfect clarity and love—and from His vantage point, He can see not just who you are, but who you're becoming and why.

Leadership expert Ronald Heifetz explains this powerfully: "Let's say you are dancing in a big ballroom... Most of your attention focuses on your dance partner, and you reserve whatever is left to make sure you don't collide with dancers close by... But, if you had gone up to the balcony and looked down on the dance floor, you might have seen a very different picture. You would have noticed all sorts of patterns."

This is exactly how God sees your identity journey. While you're caught up in immediate problems—wondering "Who am I?" in the midst of confusion and pain—God is looking down from His balcony with perfect perspective. He sees patterns you can't see, connections you miss, and purposes you don't understand yet.

From His elevated view, God sees how your wounds are becoming sources of ministry, how your struggles are developing character that reflects His own, and how everything is working together for your good and His glory.

He sees the bigger story of who you're becoming, not just the chapter you're currently living.

Most importantly, from His balcony perspective, God sees your destination—the complete restoration of your True Self. While you might feel lost in the middle of transformation, He sees the finished work and calls you by who you're becoming, not who you've been.

The Balcony Perspective teaches us: God's elevated view above your circumstances provides clarity about "Who Am Eye?" and "Whose Am Eye?" that's impossible to gain from ground level. When you learn to see your story through His eyes, you discover not only your identity but your journey has divine purpose. This sacred reflection is about working WITH God to see "Who Am Eye?" and "Whose Am Eye?" through His loving perspective above all your problems.

What God Sees Right Now About Your Identity

Using these three perspectives, here's what your Heavenly Father sees when He looks at you:

From His balcony view: He sees the courage it took to begin this journey and every moment you chose to stay engaged when it got uncomfortable. He sees a child who is becoming more like Him through the process, not someone who's failing to measure up.

Like David gazing at the stars: He sees your heart's sincere desire to know Him more deeply, even through doubt and disappointment. He sees someone who belongs to Him completely, asking the right questions and seeking the right answers.

Past all the surface ripples: He sees the tears you've shed over wounds you finally named, the bravery it took to break agreement with lies, and who you're becoming—not just who you've been. He sees your True Self emerging, and it brings Him joy.

God isn't looking at you with disappointment about how far you have to go. He's looking at you with delight about how far you've already come and who you're becoming in Him.

Preparing for What's Next: From Question to Declaration

This reflection prepares your heart for Chapter 12, where you'll actively reclaim and declare the identity God has spoken over you. The depth of your reflection determines the power of your reclamation.

When you take time to see what God has already accomplished in your identity journey, you'll step into Chapter 12 with unshakeable confidence. You'll know that the God who has been faithful in your transformation is the same God declaring your true identity. You'll move from asking "Who am I?" to declaring "I am who God says I am" with absolute certainty.

This sacred pause helps you transition from discovery to declaration—from learning whose you are to living like you know it.

Your Personal Moment of Identity Reflection (20 minutes)

Set the Environment (2 minutes):

Find a quiet place where you won't be interrupted. Have your journal and this book with you.

Worship and Positioning (3 minutes):

Begin with simple worship: "Father, I belong to You completely. Show me how You see my journey".

Reflection Questions (10 minutes):

Journal your responses to these questions – Ask Him these specific questions about your identity:

"Father, what evidence do I see of Your transforming work in my understanding of who I am?"

"How has my answer to 'Who Am Eye?' changed through this journey?"

"What do You want me to understand about whose I am, as I prepare to declare my true identity?"

"How are You preparing me to live from my True Self more consistently?"

Listening Prayer (5 minutes):

Ask: "Holy Spirit, what do You want me to know about how You see my growth?"

Don't rush. Let God speak to your heart about your identity. Write down what He shows you—these insights become crucial foundation as you step into declaring who you really are.

Final Reflection

1. **Looking back over this journey, what specific evidence do you see of God's transforming work in your identity?**

2. **How has your understanding of 'Whose Am Eye?' changed from when you started this book?**

3. **What truth about your identity is God preparing you to declare with confidence?**

Call to Action

This week, spend 15-30 minutes in quiet reflection using God's perfect prescription lenses to see your transformation journey from His perspective. Journal what He reveals about your identity growth.

Key Principle

Sacred reflection isn't delay—it's the discipline that transforms temporary insights into permanent identity change. When you see your journey through God's eyes, you gain the confidence to step boldly into who He's declaring you to be.

Scripture Foundation

"For thou hast possessed my reins: thou hast covered me in my mother's womb. I will praise thee; for I am fearfully and wonderfully made: marvellous are thy works; and that my soul knoweth right well" (Psalm 139:13-14).

"Being confident of this very thing, that he who began a good work in you will perfect it until the day of Jesus Christ" (Philippians 1:6).

Psalm 8:3-4 | Psalm 51:10 | 1 Samuel 13:14 | Philippians 1:6 | Romans 8:37 | 1 Corinthians 13:12 | Ephesians 3:10

This sacred reflection has prepared your heart for the final step in your identity journey. You've seen your transformation through God's eyes and celebrated His faithfulness. Now you're ready to boldly declare and live from the truth of who He says you are.

In Chapter 12, we move from reflection to reclamation—actively embracing and declaring the identity God has spoken over you. This sacred pause has prepared your heart to step into the fullness of who you are in Christ.

Chapter 12

Reclaim Your Identity In Christ

"But ye are a chosen generation, a royal priesthood, an holy nation, a peculiar people; that ye should shew forth the praises of him who hath called you out of darkness into his marvelous light."—(1 Peter 2:9)

From Sacred Reflection to Bold Declaration

After taking the sacred pause of reflection in Chapter 11, where you discovered the profound difference between asking "Who Am Eye?" and declaring "Whose Am I," you now move from contemplation to confident declaration. You're actively embracing and claiming the identity God has spoken over you.

Now comes the most liberating truth you'll ever encounter: It's time to stop defining yourself by what happened to you and begin living from what Christ has done for you.

When we know whose we are—beloved children of the King of Kings—we can step boldly into the fullness of who He created us to be. This doesn't come from pride, but from the deep security of being perfectly loved by the One who calls us

His own.

From False Headlines to True headlines

As you've journeyed through this book, you've learned to reject the false headlines that once defined you: 'Rejected,' 'Not enough,' 'Failure,' 'Worthless.' But now you're ready to embrace the true headlines God has written over your life: "Chosen," "Beloved," "Free," "His masterpiece."

To reclaim your identity in Christ isn't about dwelling on old labels—it's about boldly declaring the name He calls you. Today, you're not asking "Who am I?" but declaring "I am who God says I am."

My Story of Unshakeable Identity: Defining the Prisoner Who Remembered Whose He Was

Let me share a story that illustrates what it truly means to know whose you are, even when everything else is stripped away.

A missionary once journeyed to meet a man who had spent seventeen years in a Soviet prison for hosting a small Bible study. When the guards came to break his spirit with a cruel deception—forcing him to believe his family had been tortured and killed—they expected to find a defeated man ready to deny his faith.

Instead, after a night of prayer, he stood resolute.

"Last night, the Holy Spirit allowed me to hear the prayers of my wife, my children, and my brother. I know they are alive—physically and spiritually. And I will never betray my God."

When they dragged him to the prison courtyard for execution, fifteen hundred prisoners stood at their cell windows, hands raised toward heaven, singing the very song they had heard him sing every morning for seventeen years. The guards, overwhelmed, asked with genuine fear, "Who are you?"

Without hesitation, he declared, "I am a son of the living God. His name is Jesus Christ."

This man understood something profound: Your identity is not determined by your circumstances—it's anchored in whose you are. You belong to the unchanging God, and His unchanging word over your life declares you are His beloved child.

As Scripture declares: "But and if ye suffer for righteousness' sake, blessed are ye: and fear not their fear, neither be troubled; but sanctify in your hearts Christ as Lord" (1 Peter 3:14-15).

Your True Identity Declared

Here's where the journey from "Who Am Eye?" reaches its destination in "Whose Am Eye?" Scripture overflows with powerful declarations of whose you are in Christ. These aren't aspirational statements—these are present-day realities about your divine ownership:

You are God's masterpiece: "For we are his workmanship, created in Christ Jesus for good works, which God afore prepared that we should walk in them" (Ephesians 2:10).

You are a child of the Most High God: "But as many as received him, to them gave he the right to become children of God, even to them that believe on his name" (John 1:12).

You are chosen and dearly loved: "Put on therefore, as God's elect, holy and beloved, a heart of compassion, kindness, lowliness, meekness, longsuffering" (Colossians 3:12).

You are free, not enslaved: As established in Chapter 10,

"If therefore the Son shall make you free, ye shall be free indeed" (John 8:36) (referencing the detailed explanation from Chapter 10).

You are more than a conqueror: "Nay, in all these things we are more than conquerors through him that loved us" (Romans 8:37).

This is your True Self—your spiritual identity rooted in whose you are. It can never be stolen, damaged, or diminished. It can only be surrendered through unbelief or declared through faith.

The Imago Dei Restored: More than Forgiven

When you reclaim your identity in Christ, something profound happens: God's image within you—damaged by sin and wounds—gets restored.

Original Design: We were created in God's image for relationship with Him, relationship with others, and dominion over creation.

Sin's Distortion: The image became marred through disobedience, leading to shame, hiding, broken relationships, and false identities rooted in performance and fear.

Spiritual Restoration: "But we all, with open face beholding as in a glass the glory of the Lord, are changed into the same image from glory to glory, even as by the Spirit of the Lord" (2 Corinthians 3:18).

You're not just forgiven; you're being transformed back into the person God created you to be, reflecting His character more clearly each day.

Identity Received, Not Achieved

Here's the most liberating truth you'll ever discover: Your

identity in Christ isn't something you achieve—it's something you receive as a gift of grace. As Neil Anderson reminds us: we don't work for identity—we work from it. We are already accepted, already loved, already free. You don't earn His love; you rest in it.

Consider these paradigm shifts that build on the foundational truths from earlier chapters:

- Your self-worth is no longer based on achievement, but on whose approval you already have

- Your relationships are no longer driven by the need for acceptance, but by the overflow of being accepted by the One who matters most

- Your security is no longer found in circumstances, but in the unchanging character of the One who calls you His own

- Your peace is no longer dependent on control, but on trust in His sovereignty over your life

You are not what you do. You are not what you've done. You are not what's been done to you. You are whose you are in Christ—owned, loved, and claimed by the King of Kings.

The beautiful truth is this: We don't live for approval—we live from it. Our identity is secure because it was never based on us to begin with. It's based on His finished work and His faithful character as our loving Father.

Spiritual Freedom: You Are Already Free

When Christ declared you free, He didn't just forgive your sins—He broke every chain that bound you to false identities. You're no longer enslaved to:

- The need for others' approval
- The fear of rejection or failure
- The pressure to perform for love
- The lies about your worth

You're free to live as God's beloved child.

Christ's declaration over your life is this: "You are free indeed." The question is, will you choose to live like someone who belongs to the God of all freedom?

Living From Victory, Not For Victory

One of the most crucial aspects of reclaiming whose you are involves making the shift from a victim mindset to a victor reality.

Victim identity says: "I am what happened to me," "My wounds define my worth," "I'm stuck because of my past"

Victor identity says: "I am whose I am in Christ," "My wounds are part of my story, but God is writing the ending," "My past has prepared me for His purpose"

This shift doesn't happen overnight—it's a daily choice to believe God's truth about whose you are over your pain's lies about your worth.

Remember, even Jesus carried scars in His resurrected body. Your wounds don't disqualify you from belonging to Him—they often become the very place where His power is most clearly displayed through you.

The Unshakeable Foundation

Whose you are in Christ is not based on your feelings, your

circumstances, your past, or your performance. It's based on the finished work of Jesus Christ, and the unchanging character of God who calls you His beloved child.

When Jesus cried out "It is finished" on the cross, He was declaring the completion of your redemption, the establishment of whose you are, and the securing of your place in God's family forever.

This means:

- On your worst day, you still belong to Him as His beloved
- In your deepest failure, you are still owned by the One who calls you His masterpiece
- Through your greatest struggle, you still belong to the One who makes you more than a conqueror
- Despite your past, you are still chosen and claimed by the Holy One

Whose you are is as solid as the rock of ages, because it's built on Him, not you.

Your Moment of Declaration

It's time to make this personal. Right now, I want you to speak these words aloud, letting them settle deep into your heart:

"I belong to the living God. I am chosen and beloved because He says I am. I am not defined by my past mistakes, others' opinions, or my circumstances, but by whose I am in Christ—owned completely by His love, claimed forever by His grace. Today I choose to live from the truth— that I belong to the One who calls me His masterpiece, created for the good works He prepared beforehand."

This isn't positive thinking—this is declaring whose you are based on what God has already declared to be true about you.

Use the Personal Identity Declaration Worksheet in Appendix B to create your own customized identity statement that declares whose you are daily over your life.

A Life Reclaimed

The world is waiting for you to step fully into whose you are in God's kingdom. Not perfect people, but people who know whose they are. Not those who've never fallen, but those who are learning to rise in the grace of the One who owns them. Not those who have all the answers, but those who've found the Answer—the One who calls us beloved, the One who makes all things new.

When we know whose we are as God's cherished children, we can:

- Love others without needing them to complete us
- Serve from security rather than seeking significance
- Face challenges knowing our Father holds our future
- Share our story without shame, because it points to His grace
- Live with open hands, trusting His provision and timing

Your Real Story Starts Now

Go and be whose you were always meant to be—God's

image-bearer, love-carrier, hope-bringer to a world that's still learning what it means to be fully alive in Him.

The journey continues. Welcome to the beginning of everything.

But before you close this book, I want to leave you with a final truth that has sustained me through every season of ministry, every dark night of the soul, every moment when I wondered if transformation was really possible:

You are God's masterpiece, lovingly being transformed day by day into the image of Christ.

And if He's not finished with you, then the best is yet to come.

Final Reflection

Declaring Your New Beginning

1. **How has this spiritual journey changed your understanding of whose you are?**

2. **What part of your story most needs to be shared with others who are struggling to understand whose they are?**

3. **How will you continue growing in your identity as one who belongs completely to God?**

Call to Action

This week, step boldly into your reclaimed identity:

Daily Declaration: Start each morning by saying: I am

God's beloved child. I don't need to earn His love today—I already have it completely.

Identity Check-ins: Throughout the day, when you feel triggered or insecure, ask: "Which self is reacting right now? What would my True Self do here?

Evening Gratitude: Before bed, thank God for one specific way you experienced your True Self that day

Weekly Identity Review: Each week, reflect on how living from your True Self affected your relationships, decisions, and inner peace.

Share Your Story: Look for one person this week who needs to hear that they belong to God and are valuable to Him.

Key Principle

Your identity is not determined by what happened to you, what you've done, or what others think—it's anchored in the unchanging truth of whose you are: God's beloved child, perfectly known and completely loved.

Scripture Foundation

"Even as he chose us in him before the foundation of the world, that we should be holy and without blemish before him in love: having foreordained us unto adoption as sons through Jesus Christ unto himself, according to the good pleasure of his will" (Ephesians 1:4-5).

"Therefore if any man be in Christ, he is a new creature: old things are passed away; behold, all things are become new" 2 Corinthians 5:17.

John 8:36 (referencing detailed explanation from Chapter 10) | 2 Corinthians 5:17 | Ephesians 2:10 | John 1:12 | Colossians 3:12 | 1 Peter 2:9 | 1 Peter 3:14-15 | Galatians 5:1 | Romans 8:37 |

Psalm 139:13 | 2 Corinthians 3:18 | Ephesians 1:4-5

Your Journey Continues

Once you've reclaimed whose you are in Christ, the natural question becomes: How does God want to use your story to help others discover whose they are?

In 'Whose Am Eye?'—the companion to this transformative journey—we'll explore how your personal transformation becomes your mission. Your journey of healing and wholeness is just beginning to unfold into the fullness of God's purpose for your life as His beloved child.

Conclusion

The Beginning Of Your Story

"The greatest issue facing the world today, with all its heartbreaking needs, is whether those who, by profession or culture, are identified as 'Christians' will become disciples – students, apprentices, practitioners – of Jesus Christ, steadily learning from him how to live the life of the Kingdom of the Heavens into every corner of human existence."

Dallas Willard

From Identity to Mission

As we reach the end of this book, I want you to know something profound: This isn't the end of your story—this is the beginning of living as who you really are.

So we return to where we began, but now with clarity. The question isn't "Who am I?" but "Whose am I?" And you know the answer: You belong to the God who loves you completely, chose you intentionally, and is transforming you daily into His image.

But all of this—every tear, every breakthrough, every moment of surrender—has been preparing you for what comes next.

The Questions That Guide You Home

Throughout this journey, you've discovered that the deepest questions aren't about self-discovery, but about divine belonging:

Whose ocean am I sailing in, and what True North guides me home?

Whose hope am I anchored in, no matter which storms I face?

Who is the Captain of this ship, regardless of which crew member is currently at the wheel?

These are the questions that matter—the ones that anchor you in truth when storms rage, and when seas are calm.

And here's the beautiful answer that changes everything: Captain Holy Spirit is with you on every journey, in every storm, through every season. He knows these waters better than you do, and He's committed to bringing you safely home to the Father's heart.

Captain Holy Spirit: Your Faithful Navigator

You are not sailing alone. You never have been. Even when the winds of criticism howl around you, even when the storms of circumstance threaten to overwhelm your vessel, even when you find yourself drifting toward False Self patterns or hiding behind Presentable Self masks—Captain Holy Spirit remains at the helm.

He doesn't abandon ship when your Actual Self is struggling with the mess of being human. He doesn't jump overboard when your wounded patterns temporarily take the wheel. He stays. He guides. He whispers peace into the storm, and reminds you of your True North when you've lost sight of the shore.

"When thou passest through the waters, I will be with thee; and through the rivers, they shall not overflow thee: when thou walkest through the fire, thou shalt not be burned; neither shall the flame kindle upon thee" (Isaiah 43:2).

The Ocean That Never Changes

And remember this eternal truth: you are sailing in the ocean of God's unfailing love. This ocean cannot be dried up by drought, polluted by your mistakes, or frozen by others' coldness toward you. It is vast, it is deep, and it is unchanging.

As we established in Chapter 4, nothing can separate us from this love—not death, nor life, nor any other creature. The storms above may rage, but the ocean beneath remains constant. Your anchor holds not because of your grip, but because of His. Your ship stays afloat not because of your sailing skills, but because you're held by waters that cannot fail.

Your True North Never Changes

No matter which direction the winds blow—whether they're winds of success or failure, praise or criticism, abundance or loss—your True North remains constant. Your True Self, anchored in Christ's love, points steadily toward the heart of God.

When you temporarily drift East toward raw honesty about

your struggles, True North is still there.

When you get blown South into managing your image and hiding your real self, True North is still there.

When you're pushed West into old patterns of fear and control, True North is still there.

Your identity in Christ doesn't change based on which wind is currently filling your sails. Captain Holy Spirit uses every wind—even the ones that feel destructive—to ultimately guide you toward the person He's forming you to become.

The Harbor That Awaits

And remember this hope that anchors your soul: you're not just sailing aimlessly. You have a destination. There's a harbor where your ship will finally rest, where the anchor will be permanently set, where Captain Holy Spirit will say, "Well done, faithful sailor. Welcome home."

Until that day, you navigate by faith, not by sight. You trust the Captain who sees the whole journey, not just the current storm. You rest in the ocean of His love, not in the calm of perfect circumstances.

Your Story Becomes Their Hope

Discipleship begins not with what we do for Jesus, but with who we are becoming in Him. Edmund Chan puts it this way: "True discipleship is about depth before breadth—relationship before results."

But here's what moves my heart most deeply: your transformation doesn't end with you. It flows through you.

Somewhere in your sphere of influence is someone who is standing exactly where you once stood—broken, searching, asking the same desperate questions that brought you to this book. When that day comes, your story may become their hope. Your healing journey may be their invitation. Your authenticity may give them permission to stop pretending and start becoming.

This is the beautiful mystery of God's kingdom: He doesn't just heal us—He transforms us into healers. He doesn't just free us—He makes us freedom fighters. He doesn't just love us—He teaches us to love like Him.

Your New Beginning

You are God's masterpiece, being transformed day by day into the image of Christ. The very breath in your lungs is proof that He's not finished with your story yet – the best is yet to come.

The world is waiting for people who know whose they are. Not perfect people, but authentic people who are secure in God's love and willing to help others find that same security.

Final Blessing

May you live each day in the unshakeable truth that you are God's beloved child—fully known, fully loved, fully free. May your life become a living testament to the One whose image you bear, whose love surrounds you like an endless ocean, whose Spirit captains your ship all the way home.

The journey continues. Captain Holy Spirit is at the helm.

Welcome to the beginning of everything.

Appendix A

THE FOUR SELVES DISCOVERY EXERCISE

Appendix A: The Four Selves Discovery Exercise

Instructions:

For each statement below, rate how often it describes you on a scale of 1–5:

1 = Never • 2 = Rarely • 3 = Sometimes • 4 = Often • 5 = Always

ACTUAL SELF REFLECTION

The beautiful, messy reality of being human—you without filters, acknowledging both brokenness and belovedness.

Rate each statement from 1–5:

___ I acknowledge my feelings without acting on them immediately

___ I recognize both positive and negative emotions in my daily life

___ I admit when I am confused or unsure about something

___ I notice when I am responding out of fear or old habits

___ I can be honest about both my strengths and struggles

___ I seek authentic connection rather than perfect relationships

___ I'm willing to work through conflict instead of avoiding it

ACTUAL SELF TOTAL SCORE: _____

FALSE SELF REFLECTION

The wounded you, operating from fear and pain, using survival strategies that now sabotage your ability to thrive.

Rate each statement from 1–5:

___ I hide my pain by turning to unhealthy habits or distractions

___ I struggle with perfectionism or need to control situations

___ I act in ways that don't reflect who I truly want to be

___ I try to prove my worth to others through my achievements

___ I get defensive before anyone even attacks or criticizes me

___ I avoid difficult conversations because vulnerability feels dangerous

___ I feel exhausted from constantly trying to manage how others see me

FALSE SELF TOTAL SCORE: _____

PRESENTABLE SELF REFLECTION

The curated you, carefully managing impressions and avoiding vulnerability to maintain an image you think others want to see.

Rate each statement from 1–5:

___ I am very concerned with how others perceive me

___ I often act differently in public than I do in private

___ I change parts of myself to gain approval from different groups

___ I sometimes wear a "mask" to avoid showing vulnerability

___ I say what people want to hear instead of what's true for me

___ I share prayer requests that make me sound spiritual but not needy

___ I feel like I'm constantly "on stage" and can never just relax

PRESENTABLE SELF TOTAL SCORE: _____

TRUE SELF REFLECTION

The Christ-formed you, secure in God's love and naturally expressing His character through your unique personality and gifts.

Rate each statement from 1–5:

___ I feel most myself when I am in God's presence

___ I seek to grow in love, joy, peace, and other fruit of the Spirit

___ I feel aligned with who God created me to be

___ I choose honesty even when it's difficult or uncomfortable

___ I respond to situations rather than reacting from wounds

___ I love people without needing something back from them

___ I rest in my identity rather than striving to prove my worth

TRUE SELF TOTAL SCORE: ____

SPIRITUAL GROWTH INTERPRETATION GUIDELINES

Highest Score: This may be your dominant self—the version of yourself that shows up most frequently in your spiritual journey and daily life.

Lowest Score: This may be an area for spiritual growth—an aspect of yourself that could benefit from God's transforming work and intentional spiritual formation.

Balanced Scores: You may be growing in self-awareness and learning to live more consistently from your True Self through the Holy Spirit's work in your life.

NOTES FOR SPIRITUAL REFLECTION:

- Which self scored highest? What does this reveal about how you typically approach life and relationships?

- Which self scored lowest? How might God be inviting you to grow in this area through His grace?

- Are there specific situations where certain selves tend to emerge more strongly?

- How can you create space for your True Self to lead more consistently in your daily walk with Christ?

CONTINUING YOUR SPIRITUAL JOURNEY

For additional resources and ongoing support in your identity journey, please visit: www.learnlivehopejourney.info

This reflection tool is designed to increase spiritual self-awareness, not to label or limit you. All aspects of yourself are part of your journey toward becoming who Christ is forming you to be.

Remember: You are not defined by any single score or category. You are a beloved child of God being transformed by His grace into the image of Christ.

Appendix B

Personal Identity Statement Worksheet

Framework for Creating Your Identity Declaration

Creating Your Identity Declaration

As we concluded in Chapter 12, having a personal identity statement based on Scripture serves as an anchor for your soul. This simple framework will help you create a declaration of truth you can return to whenever lies start whispering.

Basic Framework

Use this simple template to create your personal identity statement:

"I am ___________ [chosen, beloved, free, etc.] because

God says I am. I am not defined by ___________ [past mistakes, others' opinions, circumstances, etc.] but by ___________ [Christ's finished work, God's unchanging love, His Word over my life]. Today I choose to live from the truth that I belong to the God who calls me ___________."

Three Simple Steps

Step 1: Choose Your Core Truth

From Scripture, select 1-2 identity truths that resonate most with your heart:

- "I am chosen" (1 Peter 2:9)
- "I am beloved" (1 John 3:1)
- "I am free" (John 8:36)
- "I am God's masterpiece" (Ephesians 2:10)

Step 2: Identify What You're NOT Defined By

Name the specific lies or circumstances you've been believing:

- Past failures or mistakes
- Others' opinions or rejection
- Current struggles or limitations

Step 3: Declare Whose You Are

Complete your statement by affirming your identity in Christ:

- "I belong to the God who never changes"
- "I am owned by perfect love"

- "I am chosen by the King of Kings"

Sample Identity Statement

"I am chosen and beloved because God says I am. I am not defined by my past mistakes or others' opinions of me, but by Christ's finished work on the cross and God's unchanging love for me. Today I choose to live from the truth that I belong to the God who calls me His masterpiece, created for good works that He prepared beforehand."

How to Use Your Identity Statement

- **Memorize it** so you can declare it anywhere, anytime
- **Speak it aloud** every morning to anchor your day in truth
- **Return to it** whenever lies start whispering or circumstances shake your confidence
- **Share it** with trusted friends who can remind you of your true identity

For Deeper Identity Formation

This basic worksheet provides a starting point for your identity declaration. For comprehensive identity formation with detailed exercises, guided reflection questions, and step-by-step processes for living from your True Self, see the **"Who Am Eye - Identity Forming Program"** companion book.

Access Information: Visit www.learnlivehopejourney.info

or contact johangreenlearnlivehopejourney.com for program details.

Key Principle

Your identity statement isn't about convincing yourself of something that might be true—it's about declaring what God has already declared to be true about you. You're not trying to become these things; you're learning to live from who you already are in Christ.

"But you are a chosen race, a royal priesthood, a holy nation, a people for God's own possession, so that you may proclaim the excellencies of Him who called you out of darkness into His marvelous light" (1 Peter 2:9).

Appendix C

Daily Identity Practices

Simple Daily Rhythms for True Self Living

These basic practices help you live more consistently from your True Self throughout each day.

Morning Identity Anchoring (3 minutes)

Before checking your phone or diving into your day, follow these steps:

1. **Breathe and Center (30 seconds)** Take 3 deep breaths and say: "Jesus, I belong to You today"

2. **Declare Your Identity (1 minute)** Speak your personal identity statement aloud or say: "I am God's beloved child, chosen and secure in His love"

3. **Set Your Intention (1 minute)** "Holy Spirit, help me live from my True Self today. Show me when other versions try to take over"

4. **Choose Love (30 seconds)** Commit to one specific way you'll reflect Christ's character today

Evening Reflection (3 minutes)

Before bed, briefly reflect on:

- Where did I experience my True Self emerging today?
- When did fear or performance take over, and how can I extend grace to myself?
- How did God's love remain constant even when my emotions fluctuated?

When You Feel Triggered (30 seconds)

Use this quick reset:

1. **Pause** - Take 3 deep breaths
2. **Ask** - "Which self wants to respond right now?"
3. **Choose** - "What would my True Self do here?"
4. **Trust** - "I belong to God and He's got this"

Weekly Identity Check-In (10 minutes)

Every Sunday evening, ask:

- Which of my Four Selves showed up most this week?
- What patterns am I noticing in my reactions and responses?

- How can I live more from my True Self next week?
- What is God teaching me about whose I am?

Scripture Memory for Identity

Memorize one verse each month:

- **Month 1:** "I am chosen and beloved" (1 Peter 2:9)
- **Month 2:** "I am fearfully and wonderfully made" (Psalm 139:14)
- **Month 3:** "I am a new creation in Christ" (2 Corinthians 5:17)
- **Month 4:** "I am more than a conqueror" (Romans 8:37)

Identity-Focused Prayer

Daily: "Father, thank You that I am Your beloved child. Help me live from this truth today rather than trying to earn Your love."

Crisis moments: "Jesus, I belong to You. My feelings don't define me—Your truth does."

For Comprehensive Daily Practices

This appendix provides essential daily rhythms for identity formation. For detailed spiritual formation practices, monthly focus areas, extended reflection guides, and community resources, see the **"Who Am Eye - Identity Forming**

Program".

Connect with our community: www.learnlivehopejourney.info

Key Reminder

You are beloved, chosen, and being transformed by God's grace. These practices are tools to help you live from that truth consistently. Be patient with yourself as the Holy Spirit does His transforming work within you.

Appendix D

Companion Journal - Reflection Tracker

WEEKLY REFLECTION QUESTIONS

Take 15-20 minutes each week to reflect on these key questions:

1. Which of the Four Selves showed up most this week?
2. Where did I experience my True Self emerging?
3. What triggers activated my False or Presentable Self?
4. How did God's love remain constant even when circumstances changed?

DAILY IDENTITY DECLARATIONS

Speak these Scripture-based truths over your life each morning:

- "I am chosen and beloved" (1 Peter 2:9)
- "I am God's masterpiece" (Ephesians 2:10)
- "I am more than a conqueror" (Romans 8:37)

- "I am free in Christ" (John 8:36)
- "I belong to God completely" (1 John 3:1)

MONTHLY REVIEW

At month's end, spend 30 minutes reflecting:

- **Identity Growth:** How has my understanding of "Whose Am Eye?" deepened?
- **Relationship Impact:** Where am I loving from overflow rather than need?
- **Next Steps:** What is God calling me toward in the coming month?

CRISIS REFLECTION QUESTIONS

When facing difficult seasons, anchor yourself with these truths:

- **In Times of Doubt:** "What truth about God's character can I hold onto right now?"
- **In Times of Rejection:** "How does God see my worth when others reject me?"
- **In Times of Failure:** "How can this experience become part of my testimony of grace?"

Resources for Continued Growth

For additional journaling resources and community support:

Website: www.learnlivehopejourney.info
Email: johangreen@learnlivehopejourney.com
Remember: Your journaling journey is sacred space

between you and God. Be honest, be vulnerable, and trust His love to meet you exactly where you are. He is transforming you day by day into the image of Christ.

Appendix E

For Those Sensing God's Call to Deeper Spiritual Formation

Resources for Continued Growth

Your Next Steps in Identity Formation

Completing "Who Am Eye?" is just the beginning of your transformation journey. Here are resources to support your continued growth in discovering whose you are and living from your True Self.

For Structured Identity Formation

"Who Am Eye - Identity Forming Program" A comprehensive 12-week curriculum for individuals, small groups, or church implementation. Includes detailed exercises, group discussion guides, and progress tracking tools.

Upcoming Books in the Series

"Whose Am Eye?" - The Companion Book. Explores how your transformed identity flows into mission and purpose. Discover your cosmic significance as God's image-bearer and how to live from authentic love rather than performance.

"Who Am Eye? - 12 Monthly Devotionals" A year-long devotional series for ongoing spiritual formation with daily reflections, monthly identity themes, and seasonal practices.

"Leading from His Presence" For those called to leadership: Learn to lead authentically from your True Self rather than performance or pressure.

"Divorced Again" Grace-filled guidance for those walking through relationship loss

"Disqualified" Grace-filled guidance for those feeling disqualified by past failures.

Community and Ongoing Support

Learn-Live-Hope Journey Community

- Website: www.learnlivehopejourney.info
- Email: johangreenlearnlivehopejourney.com
- YouTube: Learn-Live-Hope Journey channel
- Learn Live Hope Journey weekly podcast

A Personal Word

As you continue this journey, remember that discovering "Who Am Eye?" is not a destination—it's the beginning of living as who you truly are in Christ. You are not an accident. Your story matters. Your transformation has the power to impact others who are still asking the same questions you once asked.

Keep growing. Keep asking. Keep surrendering. The best is yet to come.

Blessings on your continued journey of transformation,

Dr. Johan Green

Disclaimer

IMPORTANT SPIRITUAL FORMATION DISCLAIMER

Educational and Spiritual Content Only - Not Professional Counseling or Psychological Treatment

This book, "Who Am Eye?," including all content, exercises, and The Four Selves Discovery Exercise, is provided for educational and spiritual growth purposes only. This material is **NOT** intended to be, nor should it be considered, professional counseling, psychotherapy, psychological testing, mental health treatment, medical advice, or psychological diagnosis of any kind.

PLEASE READ CAREFULLY:

Not Psychological Content:

All content in this book, including the Four Selves model (Actual Self, False Self, Presentable Self, True Self), personal stories, exercises, reflections, and self-discovery tools, represents spiritual formation concepts based on biblical principles and Christian theology. This content is **NOT** psychological theory, clinical methodology, personality testing, therapeutic intervention, or diagnostic material. Nothing in this book should be interpreted as psychological advice, psychological evaluation, or psychological treatment.

Not a Psychological Evaluation or Diagnosis:

The Four Selves model is a spiritual formation framework, **NOT** a psychological theory, personality test, clinical model, or diagnostic tool. This framework does not diagnose, treat, or evaluate any psychological conditions, personality disorders, mental health issues, or medical conditions.

Not a Substitute for Professional Care:

This book and its contents cannot and should not replace professional mental health services, counseling, psychotherapy, psychiatric treatment, or medical care. If you are experiencing mental health concerns, emotional distress, suicidal thoughts, or psychological difficulties, please seek help from a qualified mental health professional, licensed counselor, psychologist, psychiatrist, or your healthcare provider immediately.

Educational and Spiritual Purpose Only:

This book is designed solely to promote self-reflection and spiritual growth within a Christian framework. All content is based on biblical principles, theological concepts, and spiritual formation practices, not clinical psychological methods or scientific psychological research.

No Professional Relationship:

Reading this book or completing any exercises within it does not create any professional counseling relationship, therapeutic relationship, or professional service agreement between you and Dr. Johan Green or any associated ministries.

No Guarantees:

No guarantees are made regarding the accuracy, completeness, or effectiveness of any content, exercises, or reflection tools in this book. All results and insights are subjective and should be interpreted within the context of your personal spiritual journey and relationship with God.

Limitations:

The content and reflection tools in this book have not been clinically validated, peer-reviewed, or scientifically tested. They should not be used for diagnostic purposes, treatment planning, or making decisions about mental health care. Individual results may vary and should not be considered definitive statements about your personality, mental health, psychological condition, or spiritual state.

Crisis Situations:

If you are in crisis or experiencing thoughts of self-harm, please contact:

- **National Suicide Prevention Lifeline:** 988
- **Crisis Text Line:** Text HOPE to 741741
- **Your local emergency services:** 911
- **Your healthcare provider immediately**

Recommendation:

For professional support, consider consulting with licensed mental health professionals, certified counselors, or trained pastoral counselors who can provide appropriate care for your specific needs.

By reading this book and engaging with its content, you acknowledge that you understand and agree to these terms and limitations.

Dr. Johan Green is an ordained minister and holds a Doctor of Ministry degree. He is not currently licensed as a professional counselor or therapist and does not provide professional counseling, psychotherapy services, or psychological evaluations through this book or related materials.

Bibliography

Allender, Dan B. *The Healing Path: How the Hurts in Your Past Can Lead You to a More Abundant Life*. Colorado Springs: WaterBrook Press, 2000.

Anderson, Neil T. *Victory Over the Darkness: Realizing the Power of Your Identity in Christ*. Ventura, CA: Regal Books, 2000.

Bonhoeffer, Dietrich. *Life Together: The Classic Exploration of Christian Community*. New York: HarperOne, 1954.

Chan, Edmund. *The Intentional Disciple: Making Disciples the Jesus Way*. Singapore: Covenant Evangelical Free Church, 2013.

Clear, James. *Atomic Habits: An Easy & Proven Way to Build Good Habits & Break Bad Ones*. New York: Avery, 2018.

Gaylin, Willard. *Feelings: Our Vital Signs*. New York: Harper & Row, 1979.

Gunther, Randi. *Relationship Saboteurs: Overcoming the Ten Behaviors That Undermine Love*. Oakland: New Harbinger Publications, 2010.

Heifetz, Ronald A. *Leadership Without Easy Answers*. Cambridge, MA: Harvard University Press, 1994.

Jung, Carl Gustav. *Modern Man in Search of a Soul*. New York: Harcourt Brace Jovanovich, 1933.

Kaufman, Gershen. *Shame: The Power of Caring*. 3rd ed.

Rochester, VT: Schenkman Books, 1992.

Lewis, C.S. *The Problem of Pain*. New York: Macmillan, 1962.

Manning, Brennan. *Abba's Child: The Cry of the Heart for Intimate Belonging*. Colorado Springs: NavPress, 1994.

Mulholland, M. Robert Jr. *Invitation to a Journey: A Road Map for Spiritual Formation*. Downers Grove, IL: InterVarsity Press, 1993.

Nee, Watchman. *The Spiritual Man*. 3 vols. New York: Christian Fellowship Publishers, 1968.

Nouwen, Henri J.M. *Life of the Beloved: Spiritual Living in a Secular World*. New York: Crossroad Publishing, 1992.

Reimer, Rob. *Soul Care: 7 Transformational Principles for a Healthy Soul*. Franklin, TN: Carpenter's Son Publishing, 2016.

Sanders, Martin. *It's Time to Change: Breaking Free from Patterns That Hold You Back*. Nashville: Thomas Nelson, 2018.

Scazzero, Peter. *Emotionally Healthy Spirituality: It's Impossible to Be Spiritually Mature While Remaining Emotionally Immature*. Grand Rapids: Zondervan, 2017.

Smedes, Lewis B. *Shame and Grace: Healing the Shame We Don't Deserve*. New York: HarperOne, 1993.

Tauke, Beverly Hubble. *Healing Your Family Tree*. Shippensburg, PA: Destiny Image Publishers, 2005.

Terman, Lewis M., et al. *Psychological Factors in Marital Happiness*. New York: McGraw-Hill, 1938.

Willard, Dallas. *Renovation of the Heart: Putting On the Character of Christ*. Colorado Springs: NavPress, 2002.

www.ingramcontent.com/pod-product-compliance
Lightning Source LLC
LaVergne TN
LVHW041316080426
835513LV00008B/487

* 9 7 8 1 9 6 9 0 1 3 0 0 3 *